Ivy-Mantled Tower

The authors and publishers gratefully acknowledge a grant from the Marc Fitch Fund towards publication costs, a generous contribution from the late Ken Gay, President of the Hornsey Historical Society, and the very welcome support from the subscribers whose names are listed at the back of the book.

Published 2015
by Hornsey Historical Society
The Old Schoolhouse
136 Tottenham Lane
London N8 7EL
www.hornseyhistorical.org.uk

The Hornsey Historical Society was founded in 1971 to promote local history studies and conservation work within the ancient ecclesiastical and civil parish of Hornsey. These aims are achieved by means of publications, lectures, exhibitions, research, visits and walks.

ISBN 978-0-905794-53-2   © Bridget Cherry 2015

The right of Bridget Cherry to be identified as the author of this work has been asserted by her in accordance with the Copyright, Designs and Patents Act 1988.

Where not otherwise attributed, the photographs are the work of the author.

Designed by Nicholas Moll Design www.nicholasmolldesign.co.uk
Printed by Gomer Press Ltd

Ivy-Mantled Tower

A History of the Church and Churchyard
of St Mary Hornsey, Middlesex

BY
Bridget Cherry

HORNSEY HISTORICAL SOCIETY

In memory of
Joan Schwitzer and Ken Gay

Contents

FOREWORD		7
CHAPTER 1	*Introduction: The Artist's View*	9
CHAPTER 2	*Interpreting the Building:* *The Evidence for the Medieval Church*	21
CHAPTER 3	*Reformation to Restoration: From the Mid Sixteenth Century* *to the Later Seventeenth Century*	35
CHAPTER 4	*The Eighteenth Century*	47
CHAPTER 5	*The Early Nineteenth Century: The Rebuilding*	61
CHAPTER 6	*The Nineteenth Century: Canon Harvey's Church*	75
CHAPTER 7	*A Century of Change*	91
CHAPTER 8	*An Old Site with a Future?*	111
PHOTO ALBUM		121
APPENDIX: THE CHURCHYARD ECOLOGY, TREES AND PLANTS		124
PLAN WITH FEATURES MENTIONED IN THE TEXT		126
ABBREVIATIONS AND A NOTE ON SOURCES		128
INDEX		129
ILLUSTRATIONS CREDITS		132
LIST OF SUBSCRIBERS		133

St Mary's Hornsey from the south-east, by George Arnald, lithograph (LMA)

The Curfew tolls the knell of parting day,
The lowing herd wind slowly o'er the lea,
The plowman homeward plods his weary way,
And leaves the world to darkness and to me.

Now fades the glimmering landscape on the sight,
And all the air a solemn stillness holds,
Save where the beetle wheels his drowsy flight,
And drowsy tinklings lull the distant folds;

Save that from yonder ivy-mantled tow'r,
The moping owl doth to the moon complain
Of such as, wand'ring near her secret bow'r,
Molest her ancient solitary reign.

Beneath those rugged elms, that yew-tree's shade,
Where heaves the turf in many a mould'ring heap,
Each in his narrow cell forever laid,
The rude forefathers of the hamlet sleep ...

From *Elegy Written in a Country Churchyard*, by Thomas Gray (1716-1771)

Foreword

Many places in England have a parish church whose building and contents are continuing reminders of the life of past communities over the centuries. At Hornsey these links have been broken, but tangible fragments of the story survive. My interest in the subject began with practical concern about the condition of a derelict tower in a neglected churchyard, and developed with the realisation that extensive evidence survived about the changing character of the lost building of which the tower once formed a part. The tower itself had a history asking to be unravelled; some of the memorials from inside the church survived elsewhere, and an unexpected number of interesting monuments within the overgrown churchyard awaited exploration. Most surprising was the wealth of artists' views – far more than can be included in this book. Making use of both written and visual evidence, I have attempted to interpret the scattered survivals and set them in their historical context, and to pay some tribute to the many artists and photographers whose depictions of the building add so much to our understanding.

By interrogating the physical evidence one can learn much about changing interests and priorities through the centuries, about church building, religious life, commemoration, survival and preservation (of both artefacts and the natural world), in a place which was at first a small village community, but which became a part of suburban London during the nineteenth century and faced new challenges over the last hundred years. The book is not a history of the parish; the focus is on the church and churchyard. It is hoped that it will be helpful for those concerned with the care of the site and that it may also encourage others to pursue the unanswered questions and explore the wider picture of local life.

I am much indebted to the recent research undertaken by members of the Hornsey Historical Society, whose work has provided background about other aspects of Hornsey, and in particular to the late Joan Schwitzer, inspirational founder and Chairman of the HHS and the first Chairman of the Friends of Hornsey Church Tower. The research of the late Ian Murray, archivist at Bruce Castle, an early supporter of the Friends, laid foundations for future work, as did the geologist Eric Robinson whose infectious enthusiasm opened many eyes to the interest of churchyards. I owe much to the late Ken Gay, local historian and long-term Treasurer of the Friends as well as President of the HHS. He encouraged me over many years to write this book, commented on the text and suggested the title. Peter Barber, Vice President of the HHS, has also been generous with encouragement and advice. I am grateful to Joy Nichol for hunting out material in the HHS archives and for her enthusiasm during the tomb survey, to Deborah Hedgecock and the staff at the Haringey archives at Bruce Castle and likewise to the staff of London Metropolitan Archives. Father Bruce Batstone kindly allowed me to consult the archives at St Mary with St George Cranley Gardens, and Richard Hodges arranged access to these.

Special thanks are due to Ann Jones for her memories of St Mary's, to David Frith for his help over planning sources, to Bernard Nurse for allowing me to use the view he discovered in the Gough Collection, to Derek Chivers for advice on monuments and brasses, and to John Cherry for help with the medieval wills. For details about the conservation work I am indebted to Anthony Richardson, the Friends' dedicated and imaginative architect. I have also benefited from helpful comments from Trevor Cooper, Valerie Hitchman, Professor Michael Port and John Schofield and from the late Thyrza Meacock, Keith Fawkes-Underwood, John Hinshelwood, Malcolm Stokes and other members of the HHS Publications Committee, of which Janet Owen has been a most efficient and sympathetic Chair. I am most grateful for the care with which both Malcolm and Janet scrutinised the text. Laurence Marsh undertook the copyediting, Alan Nafzger was the proof reader and it has been a pleasure to work with Nicholas Moll and Leon Boothman on the design. Any mistakes that remain are my own.

The final chapter is the story of the last twenty-five years and of the work of the Friends of Hornsey Church Tower, and so is an account based on first-hand experience as well as written and visual sources. The Friends would not have got off the ground without the encouragement of the late Father Geoffrey Seabrook; the support of the Hornsey Historical Society has been vital for their survival; and the interest of the present Rector of Hornsey, Father Bruce Batstone is a valued asset. The continuing success of the Friends owes much to Peter Sanders, tireless Chair for many years, and to the support of Frances Colquhoun; both have provided generous help, information and hospitality during the writing of this book, which has been greatly enhanced by the inclusion of many of their photos and by Peter's map of the churchyard. The 'photo album' at the end of the book demonstrates how the transformation of tower and churchyard and the variety of activities undertaken have depended on the active involvement of many people. In addition to those mentioned above, this book is a tribute to the hard work and enthusiasm of Nick Allaway (Treasurer, inventor of Teddy abseiling and master of Christmas mulled wine), Vic McRae (indefatigable chief litter picker) and the late Alan Fox (invaluable gardener, keyholder and universal handyman). More recently important roles have been taken on by Stephen Brown (carer of the clocks), and Rebecca Sheldon, (current secretary). Finally I must acknowledge the work of those no longer with us: the late Hilda Johnston, Trefor Jones and Jack Schaufler, and of others, who in different ways over the past quarter century contributed much effort to give tower and churchyard a future: Thomas Cherry, Anna Cumbers, David and Daphne Dell, Tim and Sheila Denby Wood, Faith Hart, Richard Goldsmith, Jill Letten, Lachlan McDonald, Judith Ross, Adrian Skrebowski and many other helpers. This book is for them all.

Bridget Cherry
April 2015

1.1 Distant view of Hornsey Church, by J. Clennell (Brayley, Brown and Nightingale, *Beauties of England and Wales*, 1816)

CHAPTER ONE

Introduction: The Artist's View

'The footpath to the village of Hornsey is one of the sweetest walks out of the metropolis' was the opinion of John Hassell, author of *Picturesque Rides and Walks with Excursions by Water 30 miles round the British Metropolis* (1817–18). Around this time many guide books to the countryside around London drew attention to the appeal of the secluded little village lying just beyond the eastern end of the Northern Heights. The rural character of Hornsey is captured engagingly in the print by J. Clennell of 1816 [fig. 1.1].[1] Around 1800 the parish of Hornsey, like many others in Middlesex, was still largely agricultural, despite an increasing sprinkling of gentlemen's residences, convenient for those who regularly made the four-mile journey into the city.[2] Much of the population was concentrated on the western border close to the hilltop town of Highgate, and a settlement had also developed around the crossroads at Crouch End. But the special appeal for artists was the old village centre with its parish church which lay further east along the road which later became Hornsey High Street. The small church lay on the south side, just before the road dipped down towards the Lea Valley to meet the ancient route still known as Green Lanes. There were a few houses opposite, north of the road, but to the south the hedged churchyard was approached by field paths, routes which still remain today amidst the Victorian suburb [fig. 1.2].

9

1.2 Detail from the Hornsey Enclosure map, 1815 (LMA). The main road through Hornsey (later the High Street) is shown top right, crossed by the New River; the church is surrounded by the glebe land owned by the Rector

During the eighteenth century accounts of London had increasingly begun to take note of the villages on the fringes of the built-up area and of the attractions of their rural settings. When the continent was closed to travellers during the Napoleonic Wars, there was an added interest in exploring Britain and appreciating its historic sites and natural beauties. Topographical views became a staple of the London print market.[3] While the Middlesex countryside could hardly compete with the Lake District or Scottish and Welsh mountain scenery, it attracted those keen to escape for the day from the smoke-filled city. William Thornton's copiously illustrated *History of London*, first published in 1784, demonstrates the growing interest in the London countryside, as its full title indicates.[4] It describes Hornsey as 'a small but very rustic village ... it stands in a low valley but is exceedingly pleasant, having the New River winding through, which in summer time makes it truly delightful. The church is a poor irregular structure...' The appeal of Hornsey village for the visitor was no doubt heightened by the possibility of refreshment at the Three Compasses, a favourite with anglers, as its grounds extended to the banks of the New River.

1.3 Hornsey Church in Middlesex, William Thornton, *History of London*, 1784

A large number of illustrations of Hornsey church were produced from the later eighteenth century onwards. The illustration of Hornsey in Thornton's *History* [fig. 1.3] is paired with a view of the old church of St Pancras within an elegant neo-classical frame, which reflects the popularity of using such

1. INTRODUCTION: THE ARTIST'S VIEW

prints as inexpensive wall decoration as well as for book illustration. Hornsey church is shown from the south. The placing of the church in the middle distance among leafy surroundings does not allow for much detail; the artist is more concerned to show, with a little exaggeration, the way the church nestles comfortably in the folds of the hills. The 'Hilly Field' south-west of the church, mentioned in Vestry minutes, was to give its name to Hillfield Avenue.

Despite Thornton's sometimes uncomplimentary remarks, it is not surprising that parish churches were often singled out for illustration. The rural Middlesex church was generally the only stone building in its neighbourhood; its rough masonry and Gothic detail marked it as an historical curiosity among the timber-framed, weather-boarded cottages and the prim brick or stucco villas of the Middlesex countryside.[5] By the later eighteenth century, in the areas on the fringe of London, ancient stone churches were increasingly rare. The walker coming from the city might have observed that St James Clerkenwell was rebuilt in 1788, while St Mary Islington had a smart classical church already in 1751. At St John Hackney, an ambitious new building of 1791 soon led to the demolition of the older church nearby, leaving only its tower. But for the rambler who ventured over the hill to Hornsey, until 1832 the small medieval stone church remained to enhance the appeal of the rural scene.

1.4 North-west view of Hornsey Church, by Jean-Baptiste-Claude Chatelain, J. Roberts, *Fifty Small Views Adjacent to London*, 1760 (LMA)

In the mid eighteenth century visiting artists were chiefly concerned with creating a picturesque composition emphasising the rural setting. The north-west view of Hornsey Church, after a drawing by Jean-Baptiste-Claude Chatelain [fig. 1.4], was published in

11

1.5 North Prospect of the Church of Hornsey in Middlesex, 1735, drawing (Bruce Castle Museum)

1750 by J. Roberts in *Fifty Small Views Adjacent to London*, an early example of a collection of topographical views of the London countryside. Chatelain (1710–1758) was a highly regarded draughtsman and engraver of French Huguenot descent, possibly trained in France.[6] This view demonstrates his ability to create a pleasing composition, in which the church forms part of a picturesque landscape but is not given detailed architectural scrutiny. The view from the west shows the High Road on the left side with one of the bridges that spanned the New River. While the details of the tower are recognisable, the church behind is only vaguely indicated and given a misleadingly domestic appearance by the chimney on the right, added for the convenience of the vestry which occupied that part of the building.

A precocious example of an accurate view of the medieval windows is a drawing in Bruce Castle Museum prints and drawings collection dated 1735. Unusually, it shows the north side of the building visible from the High Road [fig. 1.5]. Attention to the Gothic windows is also apparent in an undated watercolour in the collections of the antiquary

1.6 Hornsey Church, view from the south, watercolour (Gough Collection, Bodleian Gough Maps 18f 32b/a)

1. INTRODUCTION: THE ARTIST'S VIEW

Richard Gough (1735–1809) [fig. 1.6]. The rustic setting is emphasised; the churchyard is separated by a rough hedge from grazing ground crossed by a footpath.

A locally based artist who produced several rough sketches of Hornsey was John Bewick (1760–95), the brother of the more famous Thomas Bewick [fig. 1.7]. His poor health was one reason why he chose to live outside London from 1789 to 1795, employed as a drawing master at the nearby Crouch End Academy, before his early death from consumption.[7]

Watercolour was increasingly popular at this time as a convenient and expressive medium for depicting the outdoor world. Various techniques existed which made it possible to reproduce artists' work for the popular market, a means of providing artists with some income.

Aquatint, a method of reproducing watercolour tones, was developed from the later eighteenth century; an early practitioner was Francis Jukes (1745–1812), a well-known topographical artist and illustrator, who often collaborated with other artists.[8] His aquatint of Hornsey, published in 1784 by I. Walker [fig. 1.8], shows the church from the south-east. This became the most popular aspect from which to depict the building; the south side offered

1.7 Hornsey Church by John Bewick, drawing (British Museum)

1.8 South-east view of Hornsey Church by Francis Jukes, aquatint published by I. Walker, 1784 (LMA)

a number of interesting features and could be sketched comfortably from the adjacent field. Jukes takes some care to indicate the variety of the windows on the south side, an indication of growing antiquarian interest in medieval architecture.

Hornsey was sufficiently well known by the end of the century to be the subject of an engraved token. On the 'Hornsey Halfpenny' of 1797, the tower is hidden in a leafy setting, an epitome of a rural retreat. Engraved tokens were popular collector's items at this time. This example [fig. 1.9] may have been produced simply as a souvenir, but the inscription on the obverse, 'a speedy and lasting peace', hints at a hidden political message at the time of the Napoleonic Wars, with rural Hornsey symbolising 'Old England'.[9]

1.9 Hornsey Halfpenny, 1797 (private collection)

Interest in English antiquities developed rapidly at this time. In 1810, *The Gentleman's Magazine*, the principal periodical reflecting antiquarian interests, included a view of Hornsey Church by Robert Schnebbelie together with drawings of a fragmentary inscription from a window, and the heraldic detail on two carvings on the west side of the tower. [fig. 1.10][10] The latter had already been noted in *The Environs of London* by Daniel Lysons, a work which raised the study of the history and antiquities of Middlesex to a new level. Lysons' brief and precise description of the church in his volume 3 (1795) was the basis of many later comments: it 'appears to have been built about the year 1500. The architecture is of that period, and the arms of Savage and Warham [two successive Bishops of London] on the tower, fix the date. The church consists of a chancel, nave, and south aisle; at the west end is a square embattled tower.'[11]

1.10 South-west view of Hornsey Church by R. Schnebbelie (*The Gentleman's Magazine*, July 1810, p. 17)

1. INTRODUCTION: THE ARTIST'S VIEW

1.11 Hornsey Church by Michael 'Angelo' Rooker (watercolour, Newport Art Gallery)

'Accuracy of representation should be combined with picturesque effect' was the advice given by the antiquary John Britton, compiler of the multi-volume *Beauties of England and Wales*, which began to appear in 1801.[12] One of the most distinguished examples of this approach among the views of Hornsey is the sensitive monochrome watercolour by Michael 'Angelo' Rooker [fig. 1.11], an artist who specialised in topographical subjects, especially medieval antiquities, presented in a picturesque manner. Rooker (1746–1801), son of an actor and engraver, had been a pupil of the topographical artist Paul Sandby and exhibited at the Royal Academy from 1779. Like many artists at this time he earned a living as a scene painter, working at the Haymarket Theatre. He produced watercolours in his spare time and on summer sketching tours.[13] Rooker's painting shows his meticulous attention to detail, showing very precisely the character of the different windows, and the textures of the building materials, yet without appearing pedantic. The painting, now in Newport Art Gallery, Wales, is undated but has been ascribed to the 1790s.

Soon after 1800, some of these intriguing ancient features were swept away when the windows of the church were modernised. An engraving of Hornsey Church of 1810 by Frederick Wilton Lichfield Stockdale shows the building from the west [fig. 1.12].[14] Stockdale, a topographical and antiquarian author and draughtsman, may have chosen the west view showing the ancient, weathered character of the building with its Gothic

1.12 Hornsey Church Middlesex, view from the west by F. W. L. Stockdale, 1810, aquatint (British Museum)

1.13 West end of Hornsey Church from the south, watercolour (LMA)

west window in preference to the more usual southern view, where the new windows would have been more apparent. These can be seen more clearly on an anonymous watercolour in the Guildhall collection at the London Metropolitan Archives [fig. 1.13], which vividly depicts the colour of the rough building materials. The new windows also appear in a tiny but detailed engraving, dated 1826, by the topographical artist George Cooke, with 'figures and effect by A. W. Collcutt R.A.' [fig. 1.14]. The low viewpoint cleverly gives the squat tower additional dignity, but by this time there were few overtly medieval features to record on the rest of the exterior.

1.14 Hornsey Church by George Cooke, engraving, with figures by A. W. Collcutt (*Views in London and its vicinity, 1826*)

1. INTRODUCTION: THE ARTIST'S VIEW

The rural appeal remained. Hassell in his *Picturesque Rides* (1817-18) commented that 'the quietude of the environs of Hornsey make it a desirable place to practise colouring from nature as few interruptions of visitors are likely to annoy the painter'.[15] The church and its setting were the subjects of several delicate and evocative lithographs of the 1820s published by the artist George Arnald from his address at 2 Weston Street, Pentonville. Arnald (1763–1841) was a landscape and topographical artist who exhibited frequently at the Royal Academy. A portrait of him at work in his studio, by his friend the antiquary J. T. Smith, is in the National Portrait Gallery [fig. 1.15].[16] Arnald enjoyed animating his pictures. A view from the south-east shows a family walking through a field with sheep [frontispiece]. In a more unusual bucolic view from the south the church is half hidden by trees and the foreground is occupied by an old man and a lively dog [fig. 1.16].

1.15 Portrait of George Arnald in his studio, by J. T. Smith (National Portrait Gallery)

1.16 Hornsey Church from the south by George Arnald (lithograph, LMA)

1.17 Hornsey Church from the north by George Arnald, lithograph (Bruce Castle Museum)

A contrasting view from the High Road includes two children bowling a hoop [fig. 1.17], demonstrating the innocent pleasures of the countryside, as well as the high ground level of the churchyard on this side, built up by successive graves through the centuries. As in many other depictions, Arnald emphasises the massive character of the tower in contrast to the rest of the building. He was also responsible for the only known views of the interior of the old church, looking east and west. These show a cosy, intimate space with plastered barrel vault, furnished according to contemporary Anglican practice with box pews, galleries, and a prominent pulpit and reredos. There were large new windows, but the south arcade is recognisably medieval, with Gothic arches on octagonal columns [figs. 1.18, 3.17].

All this was soon to be swept away. The threat of rebuilding, discussed already in the 1790s, became an additional spur to the recording of the church and its contents. The illustration in *The Gentleman's Magazine* of 1810 had been accompanied only by a brief

1. INTRODUCTION: THE ARTIST'S VIEW

note. In 1832, when demolition was imminent, the periodical published an article giving a detailed description, which demonstrated that the author had explored the interior very thoroughly, climbing the tower, and penetrating the vestry then in the west end of the south aisle, where he discovered a sculpture of an angel bust.[17] This sculpture was recorded not only in a sketch in *The Gentleman's Magazine* [fig. 1.19], but, together with some of the monuments, in a series of coloured aquatints attributed to the antiquary Thomas Fisher (1772–1836), no doubt as a precaution against their possible destruction.[18] They are notable for including relatively recent monuments as well as examples from the seventeenth century and earlier (see Chapter 4).

The Gentleman's Magazine article is signed EJC, the initials of E. J. Carlos (1798–1851), a London lawyer with antiquarian interests, who was a frequent contributor and took an active interest in topical conservation issues, such as the fate of Crosby Hall in the City, and the demolition of St Katharine by the Tower for the new docks.[19] His conclusion demonstrates how scholarly interests could be infused with the sensibility of the romantic imagination.

'Although Hornsey church was a very humble specimen of our ancient parish churches, yet inasmuch as it preserved in a tolerably perfect state its pristine character, and more especially as it was almost the last village church in the immediate neighbourhood of the metropolis, I cannot help regretting that a necessity insisted for destroying it. I should rather have seen the additional accommodation afforded by a chapel of ease, and the old church preserved as a specimen of the style of building in which our rustic neighbours in old times offered up their simple prayers.'[20]

1.18 Hornsey Church, interior looking east by George Arnald, lithograph (LMA)

This vision was not to be. The rebuilding that took place in 1832–33 and later artists' responses to it are explored in later chapters. But first, with the help of the information provided both by the artists and concerned antiquarians, the evidence for the character of the old building can be examined.

1.19 Angel sculpture (*The Gentleman's Magazine*, 1832)

---

[1] Published in *The Beauties of England and Wales*, vol. X, *Middlesex*, by John Britton and Edward Wedlake Brayley, 1816, facing p. 210.

[2] For a general history of Hornsey see the *Victoria County History of England, Middlesex*, vol. VI, ed. T. F. T. Baker, Oxford University Press and London University, 1980, pp.101–205; on St Mary's Church, pp. 173–5.

[3] Elizabeth McKellar, *Landscapes of London*, Yale University Press, 2013, esp. pp. 79–107.

[4] William Thornton, *The New, Complete, and Universal History, Description, and Survey of the Cities of London and Westminster, the Borough of Southwark, and the parts adjacent, including not only all the Parishes within the Bills of Mortality, but likewise the Towns, Villages, Palaces, Seats, and Country, to the extent of above twenty miles round; with all the late improvements and alterations*, published by Alex. Hogg, London, 1784.

[5] For medieval churches in Middlesex see *Royal Commission on Historical Monuments, Middlesex*, HMSO, 1937.

[6] *Oxford Dict. Nat. Biog. Oxford Univ. Press, article 5184*.

[7] For John Bewick and the Crouch End Academy see Nigel Tattersfield, *John Bewick: Engraver on Wood 1760–1795*, British Library, 2001; Peter Barber, 'From Grene Lettyce to Academy: A Crouch End House 1613–1882', in *People and Places: Lost Estates of Highgate, Hornsey and Wood Green*, ed. Joan Schwitzer, Hornsey Historical Society, 1996, pp. 14–37.

[8] Among his collaborators was Robert Pollard (1755–1839), best known for his sporting prints, who was buried in Hornsey churchyard. See *ODNB*, article 22471.

[9] Peter Barber, 'The Hornsey Halfpenny of 1797', *Hornsey Historical Society Bulletin* 39, 1998, pp. 11–15.

[10] *The Gentleman's Magazine* vol. 80, pt.2, 1810, p. 17. The artist was probably R. B. Schnebbelie (d. 1849). On the Schnebbelie family see H. L. Mallalieu, *Dictionary of British Watercolour Artists to 1920*, Antique Collectors' Club, vol. 1, 1976, p. 158. The Hornsey subjects were also printed as a separate portrait-shaped print by Basire.

[11] Daniel Lysons, *The Environs of London, being an Historical Account of the Towns, Villages and Hamlets, within Twelve Miles of the Capital*, vol. 3, printed for T. Cadell Jun. and W. Davies, London, 1796, pp. 46–78.

[12] John Britton, *The Beauties of England and Wales*, 1801–16.

[13] Patrick Connor, *Michael Angelo Rooker 1746–1801*, Batsford and Victoria and Albert Museum, 1984.

[14] Published in 1810 by Gaetano Testolini, an Italian engraver and printseller who had a shop at 73 Cornhill in 1802-22.

[15] John Hassell, *Picturesque Rides and Walks, with Excursions by Water, thirty miles round the British Metropolis*, 2 vols., 1818.

[16] Mallalieu, *Dictionary of British Watercolour Artists*, vol. 1, p. 64; David Saywell and Simon Jacob, *National Portrait Gallery, Complete Illustrated Catalogue*, Unicorn Press, 2004, p. 17.

[17] *The Gentleman's Magazine*, vol. 102, pt. 2,1832, pp. 11–14.

[18] Examples of these aquatints exist in the collections of the British Museum, Bruce Castle Museum and the LMA Guildhall Collection. On Fisher: *ODNB*, article 9510.

[19] Edward J. Carlos: *ODNB*, article 4689. On his contributions to *The Gentleman's Magazine* see www.worldcat.org/title/communications-to-the-gentlemans-magazine-from-1822-to-1847-by-edward-john-carlos-esqr-chiefly-marked-by-his-initials-ejc-1822-1847. Visited 10 November 2014.

[20] *The Gentleman's Magazine*, vol. 102, pt.2, 1832, p. 14.

2.1 Hornsey Church from the south-east by Thomas Prattent (*European Magazine*, 1797)

CHAPTER 2

Interpreting the Building: The Evidence for the Medieval Church

What can one deduce about the nature and date of the medieval church? While descriptions, drawings and paintings provide a picture of the appearance of the church from the mid eighteenth century onwards, it is more difficult to establish its earlier history. Land at Hornsey, including a hunting lodge at 'Lodgehill', Highgate, was among the early possessions of the medieval bishops of London, but early documentary references to the church at Hornsey are frustratingly thin.[1] The date of acquisition of Hornsey by the Bishop is unknown. It appears that it was grouped in the records with Stepney, and so was not recorded separately. It is not mentioned in Domesday Book and, like other bishop's manors in Middlesex, its name does not appear in a list of Middlesex churches made in 1244–48. The first reference is in the taxation list of 1291, where a priest at Hornsey is mentioned, but a parish church may have existed much earlier.[2]

THE BUILDING HISTORY

What evidence is provided by the artists? No plan survives, but their views indicate a church that had grown gradually to meet changing requirements, as was common with medieval parish churches. The older churches that survive in many former Middlesex

2.2 Hornsey Church from the north, engraving (Bruce Castle Museum)

villages show that by the end of the Middle Ages, the basic provision of a chancel for the clergy and a nave for the laity had frequently been supplemented by additional chapels, side aisles and a tower. The eighteenth-century views of Hornsey show that the body of the church had two parallel roofs, one covering the nave and chancel, the other covering the long south aisle which extended the whole length of the church and embraced the west tower [fig. 2.1]. On the north side there was no aisle, suggesting that the fabric of the north wall could have survived from an older building. Views that show the church from the north provide few clues, apart from the fact that there was a small north doorway, as was common in medieval churches, which survived the alterations to the windows in the early nineteenth century [fig. 2.2]. A possible relic from the early church were the small pointed niches in the spandrels of the south arcade, described and illustrated in E. J. Carlos' account of the building in *The Gentleman's Magazine*.[3] Carlos was unable to explain these, but they could have been remains of small windows, perhaps of twelfth or early thirteenth century date, which were partly blocked when the arcade was cut through the south wall [fig. 2.3]. Any early windows in the north wall are likely to have been destroyed when later windows were inserted.

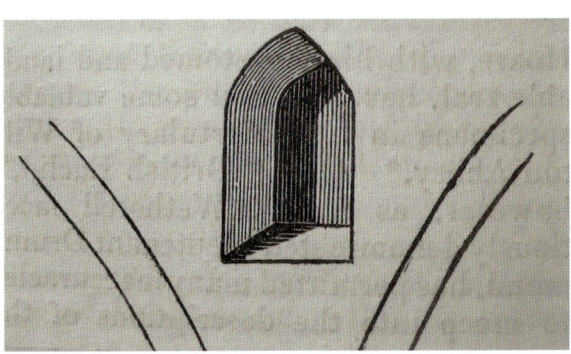

2.3 Niche in the south wall (*The Gentleman's Magazine*, 1832)

2. INTERPRETING THE BUILDING

All the medieval windows, except for the west window in the tower, were lost when large round-headed windows with plain glazing were inserted at the beginning of the nineteenth century, but their character is apparent in the older views. The windows in the north wall, two of those in the south wall, and the two east windows were all of the same type: of three uncusped lights, with mullions running up to a depressed arch protected by a hood-mould [figs. 2.4, 2.5, 2.6]. This simple type of Perpendicular tracery was a popular fifteenth century form for walls with low eaves where there was no room for elaborate upper lights. It can be seen for example in the City of London at the small church of St Olave Hart Street. The apparent uniformity of these windows suggests that a general re-windowing programme may have taken place when or after the south aisle was added. On the north side the windows are not placed centrally between the buttresses; possibly they were insertions in an earlier wall. The arrangement in the south wall is more regular, although there are two exceptions: the straight-headed three-light window at the east end of the south wall and the two-light window west of the south porch.

The polygonal projection visible between the straight-headed south-east window and the two three-light windows further west [see fig. 2.1] is probably a late addition. It is a typical arrangement for a stair to the loft over the rood screen which marked the division between nave and chancel. Its position must have

2.4 South aisle windows (detail from Gough Collection, fig. 1.6)

2.5 East wall windows (detail from Rooker, fig. 1.11)

2.6 North wall windows (detail from 1735 view, fig. 1.5)

23

2.7 East end during demolition in 1832, detail from fig. 5.9 (Museum of London)

marked a screen that ran across both the south aisle and main body of the church. The exposed brick suggested in some of the drawings of the turret may indicate an early sixteenth century date.[4] Possibly the straight-headed window next to it was made at the same time. The smaller window toward the west end of the south aisle would seem to belong to a different building programme, one which must be associated with the building of the tower (see below).

The anonymous watercolour in the Museum of London which shows the interior during demolition [fig. 2.7], suggests that the east bays of the south arcade may have been differently proportioned from the rest, with taller arches, an east respond with what appears to be a carved capital on a thin shaft, and a first column perhaps bulkier than the others, although this is not apparent in the interior view by George Arnald [fig. 2.8]. Differences between chancel and nave arches are confirmed by the observations of William Cole in the mid eighteenth century: the chancel being distinguished from the nave by 'a difference of the arch of the pillar which divides the rest of the nave from the south aisle'.[5] Such differences might have been related to traces of an earlier division between chancel and nave. But by the early sixteenth century it seems that division between chancel and nave at Hornsey was marked only by a rood screen, an arrangement characteristic of many late medieval parish churches.

The building of a chapel adjoining the chancel, later remodelled and lengthened to become a full aisle, has been found to be a common occurrence in churches in the City of London, and St Mary Hornsey may have followed a similar pattern of development.[6] The traditional division of responsibility for the upkeep of a church (the chancel by the clergy, the nave by the lay inhabitants of the parish) had been established by the thirteenth century. By the later Middle Ages lay involvement extended also to the extra additional spaces – aisles, chapels and tower. The wealth of local landowners and merchants lay behind the extensive transformation of

2.8 Detail of east end (from Arnald, fig. 1.18)

parish churches in the fifteenth century, as can be seen in the wool or cloth-producing counties of East Anglia and Somerset. Although Middlesex could not compete with such areas, bequests reveal that many enlargements and improvements to its relatively modest churches took place during this period. From the early fifteenth century onwards, local wills provide an important source of information about Hornsey Church, particularly as other types of records, such as churchwardens' accounts, have not survived.[7] What light can they shed on the building history?

The will of 'Henry Cokke of Haryngey' (Haringey, spelt variously, is an old form of Hornsey, which is used in fifteenth-century wills), was made in 1401 and proved a year later.[8] It states that he left his body to be buried in the chapel of the Holy Trinity in the church of Haryngey. He left 6s. 8d. for the church fabric and 2s. to the fraternity of St Trinity. The mention of burial in a chapel suggests that this was a distinct space, not an altar within the main body of the church. It is interesting that this reflects a personal interest in the Hornsey church and not a family tradition, as he also left money to St Pancras Church where his parents were buried and provided for masses to be said for their souls. Subsidiary altars, often maintained by a brotherhood of local people, could provide a place dedicated to prayers for the souls of the members and their families, a practice which played an important role in late medieval religion, for such prayers were believed to reduce the amount of time a soul spent in purgatory.[9] Payments would cover the costs of employing a priest for this purpose for a fixed term after a death; bequests often refer to a 'trental' of masses, that is for thirty masses, either said consecutively, or spread over a longer period. Less frequent were payments for a whole year. The later will of Robert Schapman from 1428 (an early example of a will in English) provides a bequest of 6s. 8d. 'to the kevering [covering] of the Trinity schapell of Haringey'.[10] In 1429 John Rugvale of Haringey left 20s. to the Trinity chapel and in 1452 Galfrid London provided the larger sum of 5 marks (i.e. 5 x 13s. 4d.: £3 6s. 8d.) 'ad opus capelle Scti Trinitas' towards the work of the Trinity Chapel).[11] Both the words 'kevering' and 'opus' could indicate building work. They might suggest an enlargement or improvement to the chapel which existed by 1401. In 1460 John London, a substantial property owner, left land which was to be converted into funds for 'a reparation of the Trinity ile' and other sales which would provide for 'my month's mynde and my twelvemonth mynde' (commemorative services) as well as funding a priest for a year to pray for his and others' souls.[12] The reference to the Trinity 'ile' makes it tempting to associate this work with the south aisle of the church.

The nature of the nave south arcade is known from George Arnald's early nineteenth-century lithographs [see figs. 1.18, 2.8 and 3.17]: pointed arches with chamfered mouldings, supported by octagonal columns with moulded capitals. Such details are characteristic of later medieval work in many parish churches. Octagonal columns were favoured especially in the fourteenth century (there are examples at St Mary Lambeth and All Hallows Tottenham), but would not have been the most up-to-date design by the mid fifteenth century. By then the characteristic Perpendicular Gothic pier was a slim structure with four attached shafts (as used, for example, in the arcades of St Dunstan Stepney). This might support the suggestion that the fifteenth century bequests to Hornsey assisted with remodelling (a new roof and windows?) rather than new building. The simple forms of the south arcade and the lack of a clerestorey (upper windows) differ from the more sophisticated aisles of the Perpendicular period surviving or recorded at, for example, the parish churches of Stepney and Hackney or, in the City, at St Andrew Undershaft and St Giles Cripplegate. In the 1460s, the new tower being built at Fulham had a respond of the quatrefoil pier type. Compared with other fifteenth century building in and around London, the work at Hornsey was old-fashioned, reflecting modest resources and ambitions on the part of the donors.

THE TOWER

While the appearance of chancel, nave and aisle have to be imagined from records, the tower, although considerably altered, survives to be studied on the ground [fig. 2.9]. The tower stood west of the church, and

2.9 Hornsey tower, from south-east

was linked to it by arches in its east and south walls. The south arch is now blocked but visible inside the tower [fig. 2.10]. The floor inserted in 1833 makes the arches appear misleadingly low; their bases can be seen in the basement created below, which is some sixteen inches lower than the original ground floor of the medieval building. In keeping with the octagonal columns of the south arcade, the responds to both south and east arches are shaped as half octagons [fig. 2.11]. The two pairs of arch mouldings and bases,

2.10 Tower interior, south-east corner

although very worn, appear similar and it would seem likely they were constructed at the same time. The south arch suggests an already existing south aisle. Did it belong with the construction of the south aisle, or was it an afterthought, but built to match the rather old-fashioned architectural detail of the arcade? A possibility is that some of the worked stone is reused. John Norden's *Speculum Britanniae*, published 1593, notes that 'the church of Harnsey is supposed to be built with the stones that came from the old ruins of Lodgehill, (i.e. the bishop's lodge at Highgate).[13] Norden describes Lodgehill as 'old and overgrown', with heaps of rubble. It was an obvious useful source of building material, and would have been an inexpensive way for the bishop to fund the building programme.

2.11 Tower basement, south-east corner, arch bases

2.12 Angel capital, south tower arch, east side

2.13 Angel capital, south tower arch, west side

THE PUZZLE OF THE ANGEL CAPITALS

Just as the windows at the west end of the aisle differed from those further east, the capitals of the south arch between tower and aisle, visible inside the tower, differ from those of the lost south arcade. They are distinguished by carved angels bearing shields, a popular late medieval device [figs. 2.12, 2.13]. The worn Reigate stones used for the arch itself have been partly repaired, probably in 1833, but the capitals, of a rather better quality stone, appear original. Does this extra embellishment suggest that this end of the aisle, or the tower itself, may have had a special function, or could it have been simply a chance to make use of some material from Lodgehill? The description of the two tower arches by the antiquary E. J. Carlos is intriguing. He mentions that the *east arch opening from the tower into the nave of the church* had a 'handsome moulded architrave springing from two corbels representing angels bearing plain shields', and he notes that the *south arch from the tower to the south aisle* had similar corbels. That implies two sets of angel capitals. Or did Carlos confuse his notes? Close observation of the capitals of the east arch, now partly concealed by the wall that later filled in part of the archway, confirms that these capitals might have had carving which has been hacked off [fig. 2.14].

HOW OLD IS THE TOWER?

The dates of both the south aisle and its end bay, and the ground floor of the tower, remain uncertain, but the wills point to work in the fifteenth century. By this time church towers were widespread, a means of expressing the status and significance of a parish of any standing. Aspirations for a tower at Hornsey certainly existed in the fifteenth century. John Rugvale, whose will of 1429 has already been mentioned, not only left 3s. 4d. for the fabric of the church but another 3s. 4d. specifically 'ad facturam campanile' – for the building of a bell tower. But this building project was a long one, for in 1480 Thomas Basse left 5 marks (£3 6s. 8d.) for 'the making of the stepull of haringye', and there were further gifts even later: 6s. 8d. for the steeple from John Hill in 1505; another 6s. 8d. 'for the byldyng of the stypyll' in 1517 from Robert Lolocks; 6s. 8d. 'ad opus campanile' from William Thomson in 1518.[14] (The word steeple was used interchangeably with tower; it does not imply a spire.) Elsewhere in England, for example in Suffolk, there is evidence that it was common for the building period of a tower to stretch over several decades, funded gradually by bequests from parishioners.[15] At Hornsey it appears that the tower was the last part of the building programme to be completed.

2.14 Capital, tower, east arch, north side

THE BUILDING MATERIALS

Externally the tower appears to be of stone, but this is only a facing for a structure of red brick, visible internally, especially on the west and north walls of the present basement and in the stair turret [fig. 2.15]. The use of brick became increasingly common in and around London during the fifteenth century, but not until the early sixteenth century was it considered sufficiently smart to be left exposed as a material in its own right. A later fifteenth century date for the construction would be plausible. Good building stone was not readily available in Middlesex. The facing stone is of rubble, of many different types, incorporating later repairs in Portland stone, but also the dark conglomerate stained by iron, sometimes called 'ferricrete', that is found locally in Middlesex [fig. 2.16]. It can be seen in other medieval churches, for example St John the Baptist Pinner. The walls are noticeably different from the more uniform Kentish rag that was used widely in the fifteenth century, both in the City of London and for more ambitious village churches, such as the tower remaining from St Augustine Hackney. Superior freestone that could be cut to shape was needed for the tower arches and windows. These details were of Reigate stone; this weathers badly when exposed and has been much repaired.

2.15 Tower basement, interior brickwork

2.16 Tower, exterior stonework at ground level    2.17 Tower basement, fireplace in north wall

In the north wall, now at present basement level, is a curiosity, a fireplace with stone four-centred arch; its flue rising through the thickness of the wall [fig. 2.17]. It appears to be an original feature and suggests that the ground floor of the tower was intended to have some practical use. It might have provided heating for a space used as a vestry or church room, entered from the main part of the church. Many churches have west doorways, used for processions and important ceremonies, but at Hornsey the church only had north and south doors, so that there would have been no conflict in using the ground floor of the tower for a special purpose.

Early antiquarians dated the tower and church to c. 1500, because of the heraldry on two carvings on the exterior of the west wall of the tower, sited just above the west window [fig. 2.18]. Here angels appear again, each holding a shield. The older views show that these carvings were originally larger, with whole figures of angels [fig. 2.19].[16] The heraldry, clearly visible in the eighteenth century, was identified as the arms of two London bishops: on the left Thomas Savage Bishop of London in 1496–1501, Archbishop of York from 1501, and on the right William Warham Bishop of London in 1501–03, later Archbishop of Canterbury. Only the figure on the right (southern side) is now legible; the swords in saltire on the dexter side are the arms of the Bishop of London, the sinister side had the personal arms of the Bishop; Warham's arms had three scallops beneath a goat's head erased; the latter appears to have been mistaken by the artist as a star.[17] The inclusion on Savage's shield of the archbishop of York's pallium implies that it dates from after 1501 when he became Archbishop. Both carvings must have been erected together, before 1503, while Warham was Bishop of London. The carving, though very worn, appears remarkably delicate, with a finesse not found on the

2.18 Tower west wall, exterior

29

2.19 Carvings on west wall, detail from Gentleman's Magazine 1810 (see fig. 1.10)

angel capitals [fig. 2.20]. However they prove neither the start nor the completion of the tower, only that by this date the tower had reached this height and that these bishops may have assisted with its funding. As Lord of the Manor the Bishop of London would have had a lay as well as a clerical responsibility towards the building.

Some fragmentary lost evidence suggests that other donors to the church may also have been commemorated. An unsolved puzzle, perhaps indicating another donor, is the record of a loose carving of an angel bust with a shield with a coat of arms, which E. J. Carlos discovered in the vestry in the west bay of the south aisle, and illustrated in his article of 1832. It was also drawn by Fisher [fig. 2.21].[18] The carving had earlier been described by Lysons, who commented that the arms on the sinister side, i.e. the right side on the drawing (azure, a chevron or between three besants) were also to be seen in the windows of the south aisle.[19] The drawing suggests quite elaborate carving comparable to the angels with shields on the exterior, but close comparison is not possible as the carving has disappeared.

To appreciate the tower in its pre-nineteenth century form one needs to discount the later alterations dating from the rebuilding in 1833, when the building was transformed into a taller structure by the addition of a new belfry above the clock floor and ringing chamber. Several of the old views emphasise the bulk of the tower, showing that it was three-storeyed, with a north-west stair turret crowned by a weathervane, and a plain parapet [fig. 2.22]. A tower with corner turret rising above the level of the top parapet was a popular design from the later fourteenth century onwards, especially in the London region and in Kent. The design does not appear ambitious when compared with regional types in wealthier counties, but it seems to have been acceptable to the clerical establishment as it was used both for St Mary Lambeth, the church outside the gates of

2.20 Tower west wall, southern angel carving with arms of the Bishop of London (photographed 2009)

2.21 Loose angel carving, recorded before 1832, lithograph attributed to Thomas Fisher (LMA)

2. INTERPRETING THE BUILDING

2.22 Hornsey Church from the west, engraving after William Capon (Bruce Castle Museum)

the archbishop's palace, and for the fifteenth century parish church at Fulham, close to the Bishop of London's principal country residence. The type may originally have been inspired by military architecture (Caernarvon Castle had towers with upstanding turrets in the late thirteenth century) but by the fifteenth century it appears in many contexts, for instance at Oxford colleges and abbey gatehouses. It became widespread in the London area: good examples of four stage towers are All Saints Edmonton, St John the Baptist Pinner, both fifteenth century, and St Augustine Hackney, probably of c. 1500 (where the turret has been truncated). A smaller example is the gatehouse to Barking Abbey, built with an upstanding stair turret providing access to an upper chapel.

At Hornsey the pre-1832 views show a three-stage tower. The spiral turret stair is on a surprisingly generous scale when compared with other late medieval church towers in the region. The stairs have steps about 32–33 inches (81–84cm) wide, which continue at the same width up to the present clock floor. The scale suggests an ambitious building, intended to have generous provision for bells and bell ringers. Old views show that the upper room had only a minimal south window before the alterations of 1833, and a domestic use seems unlikely. It was probably always used as the bell-ringing chamber, with the bells housed on the level above. The old views show modest belfry windows, low and square-headed. Interpreting these upper levels is difficult, as there were considerable alterations in the later eighteenth century, when new bells were installed (see Chapter 4). The description of the church by E. J. Carlos in 1832 suggests there was some evidence that the tower was incomplete; perhaps an additional storey had been intended. This might have created a rather grander tower of four stages (as at Fulham and Lambeth) with a series of taller floors. Some of the artists' views indicate that the parapet may

31

have been of brick, an inexpensive curtailment of grander hopes. Whatever the original intention, by the 1540s the tower was sufficiently complete to function as a bell tower, for the inventory of church goods made in 1552 during the reign of King Edward VI (discussed below) records that there were three bells and a small sanctus bell (a handbell), a respectable number, although fewer than in some larger Middlesex churches.[20]

CHURCH PRACTICES BEFORE THE REFORMATION

The wills already mentioned provide glimpses of how the church was used before the reforms of the sixteenth century. The function of medieval wills was not only to arrange for the disposal of possessions and wealth, but also to give instructions for burial and commemoration. Six wills from the period 1401 to the 1530s specify burial in the church, including, as we have seen, in the Trinity chapel. In 1480 Thomas Basse requested burial 'before the rood', while Robert Turvey wished to lie 'where my father lyeth buryed'.[21] Six other testators asked to be buried in the churchyard. Wills often specify the commemorative masses that were to be said for the benefit of the deceased. Robert Schapman in 1428 left 12d. to the High Altar and a 'competent saleri' (the amount is unspecified) for a whole year to a priest who would 'singe for me and all christen soules' and Thomas Basse made a similar arrangement. A popular commemoration was the trental, a set of 30 requiem masses. Robert Lolocks, in 1517 and William Alforth in 1533 both left money for this purpose, and William Alforth also asked to 'be kept on the bede roll', to be remembered in the daily prayers of the church.[22] Such practices were often intended to benefit not just the donor but also his family and others. John London, probably the most significant fifteenth century donor to the church, who in 1460 left houses to be sold for the Trinity aisle, and money for a new bell, specified that other property should be sold 'to bring me to earth' and 'to keep my month's mynde [a special service one month after the death] and my twelvemonth mynde … and to pay a priest for a year to pray for Geoffrey London, John London and all Christian souls'. Any money left over was to be spent on the 'highway under the park'. In 1505 John Hill, who lived in a house on Muswell Hill, left 3s. 4d. for an obit (prayers) to be kept in the parish church for the souls of his parents, friends and all Christian souls (as well as 3s. 4d. to the highway 'under Haringey Park side'). Lesser donations to assist in the functioning of the church were also frequent, especially money towards lights for the high altar (payments range from 8d. to 3s. 4d. and 6s. 8d.). John Hill left 20d. for 'two torches', types of very large candle used in processions.[23]

None of the wills mention permanent memorials, but two small brasses survive to show that Hornsey, like other churches in the London region, included examples of the modest monuments that had become popular among merchants and lesser landowners by the fifteenth century. Richard Ruggevale (very likely a relation of the John Rugvale, see p. 25) who left money for building the tower, and his two wives are commemorated by a simple Latin inscription attributed to the early fifteenth century: 'Hic iacent Ricus Ruggevale et Isabella ac Alicia uxores eius quor aiabs ppicietur deus Ame' ('Here lie Richard Ruggevale and Isabella and Alicia, his wives, on whose souls may God have mercy, Amen', the standard prayer at the end being in typically abbreviated form).[24] This brass is now at St Mary with St George Hornsey, as is a more unusual small brass commemorating the infant John Skevington, who is shown as a swaddled babe, a device that was popular in the early sixteenth century and is found on a number of brasses elsewhere [fig. 2.23].[25] Below the little figure is an inscription in English: 'Jesus Christ, Mary's son, Have mercy on the soul of John Skevington', which was formerly accompanied by a coat of arms. While the Rugvales were a local family already in the fifteenth century, the Skevington (or Skeffington) connection appears to have started with Sir John Skeffington, a London alderman, who before his death in 1525 established an estate at Hornsey.[26] The coat of arms associated with the brass, recorded on the early nineteenth century drawing but now lost, links it to the family whose seat was Skeffington Hall at Skeffington, Leicestershire.[27] William Cole in the mid eighteenth century noted that the brass was sited below the arch between the chancel and the south aisle; burial near the main altar was a mark of superior status.

2.23 Brass to John Skevington, aquatint attributed to Thomas Fisher (LMA)

THE MID SIXTEENTH CENTURY

The reforms instigated under Henry VIII and carried further under Edward VI abolished prayers and masses for the dead and simplified the ritual accompanying church services.[28] The inventories of church goods made in 1552 by the commissioners of Edward VI provide fascinating snapshots of churches at a time of rapid change.[29] The situation in rural parishes was very much simpler than in the City of London, whose parish records reflect the upheavals over the years of Henry VIII's reforms, listing church goods sold, as well as those which remained.[30] Compared with the rich furnishings of the city churches, the Hornsey list is simple, but revealing in its mixture of old and new liturgical equipment.[31]

Mention of a single silver and gilt chalice and a copper and gilt paten implies that no other altars were then in use – fraternities and guilds had been abolished in 1547 and superfluous plate had been confiscated. Then comes a list of vestments, which were still permissible, although with the disappearance of extra mass priests and the abolition of most of the holy days commemorating the saints, their use would have been limited: one cope of baudekyn (a brocade) a second cope of green and blue silk; six colourful sets of vestments (mostly blue with gold decoration) made of velvet, satin or silk, and three further 'old' vestments.

The metal (latten) objects are traditional: twelve bowls to set candles on (these may have been displayed on the rood screen), a censer, two great and two little candlesticks, and a cross and a basin. Among the miscellaneous list of 'Bells with divers other things' are: 'three bells in the church steeple' and a small sanctus bell (rung during the mass but by then prohibited); a table (which would have been a replacement for the stone altar proscribed in 1550), three chests (for vestments perhaps?) and a poor box; surplices, a black silk hearse cloth and various objects associated with processions: two green silkcross cloths (used on cross shaped banners), two streamers (another sort of banner), one of painted canvas, one of green silk; four banner cloths, two of blue silk and two painted; six banner staves; and finally two torches, perhaps successors to the ones given by John Hill fifty years earlier – altogether enough to suggest that there would have been colourful displays on the traditional festivals of the liturgical year, occasions which the Edwardian reformers were now keen to abolish.

In general, radical changes were delayed by the death of Edward, followed by the reintroduction of Catholic practices under Mary in 1553. After 1558 the Elizabethan settlement adopted a less extreme form of Protestantism. Processions and the use of vestments were discontinued. Images were condemned as superstitious and churches no longer had a Rood (the Crucifixion standing on the rood screen). At Hornsey the rood screen disappeared, we do not know when; only its stair turret remained, projecting from the south aisle, possibly a sixteenth-century addition made only just before the Reformation.[32] The church bells mentioned in the inventory survived, to be given a new lease of life with the development of change ringing in the seventeenth century. The one liturgical object that was not abolished was the font. The unusual story of the Hornsey font will be told in the following chapter.

---

[1] Lodgehill: *VCH Middlesex*, vol. VI, p. 140. For early references to Hornsey Church, ibid. p. 107.

[2] A priest is recorded in 1302 (ibid.); named rectors, starting in the early fourteenth century, are listed in Newcourt, Repertorium, 1708, reproduced in J. H. Lloyd, *The History, Topography and Antiquities of Highgate*, 1888, pp. 88–9.

[3] *Gentleman's Magazine*, vol. 102, pt. 2, 1832, p.13.

[4] Surviving brick stair turrets of this type can be seen at All Hallows Tottenham and St Dunstan Stepney.

[5] BL Add MSS 5836 fo. 74ff.

[6] John Schofield, 'Saxon and Medieval Churches in the City of London: A Review', *Trans. London and Middlesex Archaeol. Soc.* 45, 1994, pp. 23–146, esp. pp. 46–8.

[7] LMA Guildhall Collection 9171 (bound volume of London Commissary Court wills up to 1514); vol. 9 (wills from 1515–21), vol. 10 (wills from 1522–39).

[8] Guildhall 9171/2 fo.17.

[9] Jessica Freeman, 'The Religious Fraternities of Medieval Middlesex', *Trans. London and Middlesex Archaeological Soc.* 62, 2011, pp. 205–50.

[10] *Fifty Early English Wills, AD 1387–1439*, ed. F. J. Furnivall, Early English Text Society, 1882.

[11] John Rugvale: Guildhall 9171/3, fo.223v; Galfrid London: Guildhall 9171/5 fo.91.

[12] John London: Guildhall 9171/5, fo.309.

[13] John Norden, *Speculum Britanniae, an historical and chorographical description of Middlesex and Hertfordshire*, 1593.

[14] Thomas Basse: 9171/6 fo.311; John Hill, 9171/8 f.228; Robert Lolock and William Thompson, London Commissary Court 9, fo. 62v.

[15] See, for example, *Wills of the Archdeaconry of Sudbury, 1439–1474*, ed. P. Northeast, Suffolk Record Society XLIV, 2001; vol. II, ed. P. Northeast and H. Falvey, ibid. LIII, 2009

[16] *The Gentleman's Magazine*, vol. 80, pt. 2, 1810, p. 171.

[17] T. Woodcock and S. Flower, *Dictionary of British Arms*, vol. 3, 2009, p. 420; *Memorials of Old Middlesex*, ed. J. Tavernor Perry, London, 1909, p. 52.

[18] *The Gentleman's Magazine*, vol. 102, pt. 2, 1832, p. 13.

[19] Lysons suggested that the sinister side was similar to the arms of the Scorey family; and that the arms on the dexter side were 'borne by Otoft and Jennings'. Lysons, *Environs*, vol. 3, p.54.

[20] On medieval bells see H. B. Walters, *Church Bells of England*, Oxford, 1912.

[21] Basse 9171, 6, fo.311; Turvey: 9171 fo.311.

[22] Alforth: London Commissary Court, 10 fo.210v.

[23] John Hill: 9171/8 fo.228.

[24] H. K. Cameron, 'The Brasses of Middlesex, Hornsey', *Trans. London and Middlesex Archaeol. Soc.* 18, 1977, pp. 309–14. Cameron read the name as 'Ruggenale', but the will of John Ruggevale suggests an alternative reading.

[25] John Page-Phillips, *Children on Brasses*, Monumental Brass Society, London, 1994.

[26] *VCH Middlesex*, vol. VI, p. 108.

[27] The drawing misleadingly has transformed the three bulls' heads of the Skeffington arms into three crab-like creatures in the lower left quarter.

[28] On liturgical changes during this period see Beat Kümin, *The Shaping of a Community: The Rise and Reformation of the English Parish c. 1400–1560*, Aldershot, Scolar Press, 1996.

[29] E. Duffy, 'The End of It All: The Material Culture of the English Medieval Parish Church and the 1552 Inventories of Church Goods', in *The Parish in Late Medieval England*, Harlaxton Medieval Studies XIV, 2006, pp. 381–99.

[30] H. B. Walters, *London Churches at the Reformation*, London, 1939.

[31] Hornsey inventory: TNA E315/498. The Edwardian inventories for some of the Middlesex parishes (but excluding Hornsey) are discussed by Laurence S. Snell in *Trans. London and Middlesex Archaeol. Soc.* 25, 1974; 26, 1975; 27, 1976; 29, 1978; 31, 1980.

[32] Evidence elsewhere indicates that many rood screens were installed as late as the early sixteenth century. See E. Duffy, 'The Parish, Piety and Patronage in East Anglia', in *The Parish in English Life 1410-1600*, ed. Katherine L. French, Gary G. Gibbs and Beat A. Kümin, Manchester University Press, 1997.

3.1 The early sixteenth century font now in St Mary with St George, as centrepiece of the 2009 exhibition about St Mary's. In the background, rubbing by Derek Chivers of the alabaster tomb to George Rey.

CHAPTER 3

Reformation to Restoration: From the Mid Sixteenth Century to the Later Seventeenth Century

The churchmen of the Reformation swept away furnishings and images which were regarded as idolatrous, seeking to introduce simpler forms of religion directly dependent on the Bible. But Protestant reformers accepted the Sacrament of Baptism, and so medieval fonts were spared the destruction that was the fate of altars and images.

The font from St Mary's Hornsey was preserved, and has survived, despite a turbulent recent history. It was moved into the rebuilt church in 1833, but the new Victorian church of 1889 acquired a grander font and in 1908 the old font was given to St George, Priory Road, a new church for the growing suburb half a mile to the west. This church was gutted by a bomb in World War II. The shattered font was pieced together and after the war installed in the new St George, built a short distance away in Cranley Gardens [fig. 3.1].[1]

The font is well recorded. William Cole noted in the mid eighteenth century that the 'small neat font' stood in the south aisle – hence its absence in Arnald's interior views which show the nave of the old church.[2] A position near the main door was a traditional

35

site for the font, symbolising entrance into church membership. The Hornsey font appears to be contemporary with the completion of the west tower of the parish church in the early sixteenth century. Octagonal fonts were popular from the fourteenth century, and new fonts formed a part of the widespread rebuilding and refurbishing of parish churches which took place in the later Middle Ages. Out of some 180 known medieval fonts in Essex, for example, half date from the fourteenth to the early sixteenth centuries.[3] Such furnishings commonly made use of the architectural motifs of Perpendicular architecture. Some fonts have ambitious sculptural decoration, but the Hornsey example is relatively simple. Each face of the octagonal bowl is carved with a square containing a quatrefoil in which is set, alternately, a flower and a shield. The sloping section below has a floral ornament on each face, and the octagonal stem is defined by angle shafts which flank trefoiled arches. Details of this type were common, although on individual fonts they are used in different combinations, implying that each font was a separate commission, not a standard product. The closest comparison in the London area is the font in the chapel of St Peter ad Vincula in the Tower of London, which is contemporary with the rebuilding of the chapel in 1519–20.[4] This has the same type of pointed quatrefoil on the bowl, but no other carving, and a plain stem.

The flowers on the Hornsey font are carved in relief, but the shields have flat faces, and several of them are incised with the device of a lozenge divided by a saltire cross. This apparently insignificant detail raises interesting questions [fig. 3.2]. The decoration is not recent, as the incised lines appear on the drawings of the font made in the early nineteenth century [fig. 3.3]. While it is not unusual for church furnishings to be personalised to indicate a donor, these scratched lines are crude in comparison with the rest of the carving and look like an afterthought. The pattern of a lozenge intersected by a saltire cross is strikingly similar to the heraldry shown on the monument to Robert Harrington who died aged eighty, having been rector for fifty years [fig. 3.4]. Harrington had an interesting early life.[5] His appointment in 1560 by Edmund Grindal, Bishop of London from 1559, followed the dismissal of his predecessor Robert Willarton who, as rector under Queen Mary from 1556, was a supporter of the Catholic tradition. Harrington, in contrast, is known to have been associated with a number of active reformers who were imprisoned during Mary's reign. Like other reformers, including Grindal, he went into exile, and lived in Frankfurt until it was safe to return. He did not follow the Calvinist supporters of John Knox who moved to Geneva, and may have met Grindal abroad. Grindal was living in Strasbourg, but visited Frankfurt in an effort to reconcile the different groups.[6] The radical nature of the changes within the church hierarchy at this time is demonstrated by the fact that Harrington was among 294 clergy appointed by Grindal during his first two years of office – over half the clergy for whom he was responsible in his diocese.

3.2 Font detail showing scratch carving on shield

3.3 Font, early nineteenth century drawing attributed to Thomas Fisher, (LMA)

3.4 Wall monument to Robert Harrington, Rector of Horney, 1610, rubbing by Derek Chivers

Could the shields on the font originally have borne some decoration, perhaps referring to St Mary, to whom the church is dedicated, which the new rector thought best to remove and replace with his own device? Perhaps he was encouraged by the carved flower on the other panels which fortuitously also appears on his own arms. Harrington's monument (now at St Mary with St George), is a stone tablet with a well-carved coat of arms and an inscription inset below, which notes his exceptionally long term of service of fifty years. Its position opposite the pulpit, recorded in later descriptions, was an apt position for the memorial of a Reformation preacher, in contrast to the medieval custom of placing priests' monuments within the chancel. Its Roman lettering shows the influence of the classical style which was beginning to make an impact on older medieval traditions [fig. 3.5].

THE CHURCH IN THE SEVENTEENTH CENTURY: A VARIETY OF MONUMENTS

Because of the absence of churchwardens' accounts we know little about Hornsey Church in the later sixteenth and early seventeenth century, apart from details of some of the monuments. The Hornsey examples from this period demonstrate how various these could be. The Protestant tradition did not prohibit monuments provided there were no unacceptable inscriptions, such as requests for prayers for the

3.5 The Harrington and Lant monuments on the column opposite the pulpit (detail from fig. 3.17)

37

soul of the departed. Such prayers were reasons for the destruction of many older brass memorials. But brasses continued to be popular into the seventeenth century, especially in the London area. At Hornsey, a small brass inscription survives, to two infant sons of William Priestley, both called Thomas, who died in 1613 and 1615. Lysons noted that this was in the south aisle; it was discovered later in the crypt of the building of 1833 when this was demolished [fig. 3.6].[7] The unusual feature of this brass is one that would not have been visible to the spectator: it is a 'palimpsest', or reused piece, with engraving on its reverse side. This shows a fragment of a larger design, with three pairs of carefully depicted feet of civilian figures, made lively by vigorous cross-hatching, as was the fashion in brasses of this period. The detail of the lace-up shoes, and the round plinths on which they are standing, can be paralleled in other brasses of around 1600, indicating that this piece was a waster from the workshop, not salvage from a pre-Reformation memorial [fig. 3.7].[8]

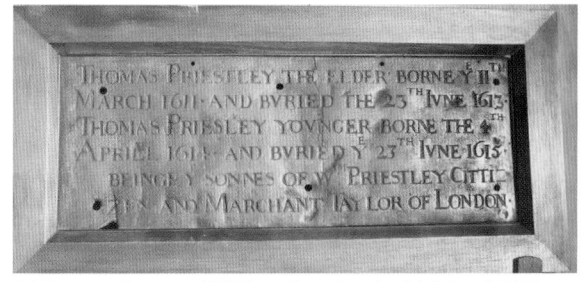

3.6 Brass to the sons of William Priestley, died 1613 and 1615 (Historic England)

William Priestley died in 1620; from his will we know that he was a London merchant, but brought up in Manchester. He asked to be buried at All Hallows Bread Street in the City, where his two wives lay, but he established his family at Hornsey, leaving his house to his daughter.[9] From a reference of 1619, it appears he took over the house 'in Frees Lane' (now Middle Lane) previously occupied by the Skevington family.[10] His will records that he left money to the Merchant Taylors for the benefit of the poor in Manchester, and for eight poor men, of whom four were to be chosen from the parish of Hornsey.

The shared loyalties to place of origin, place of work in the City and home in Hornsey is a theme common to many Hornsey memorials. It is reflected also in the very different monument to the merchant George Rey, a massive alabaster slab with shallow incised outlines of the nearly life-size figures, boldly depicted. They show Rey, his two wives and

3.7 Palimpsest back of the Priestley brass, rubbing by Derek Chivers

3.8 Alabaster monument to George Rey, c.1600, print from a drawing by Thomas Fisher (Bruce Castle Museum)

3.9 Upper part of the George Rey monument

son [figs. 3.8, 3.9].[11] In the eighteenth century the monument is recorded as standing against the wall in the south aisle.[12] In the medieval period finely carved alabaster from the Midlands was widely transported, but the simpler very large engraved alabaster slabs which continued to be popular in the sixteenth and seventeenth centuries are confined to the Midlands region where alabaster was quarried. The Rey slab has been compared with similar Staffordshire slabs of the late sixteenth century.[13] While it was not unusual for London-made monuments to be exported to other counties, it is exceptional for such a distinctly regional type of monument to be found so far from its origin, and it is unique in the London area.[14] The explanation must be Rey's family connections. His will reveals that he was born at Brewood, Staffordshire. It requests 'a stone to cover my grave to the value of 40s'.[15] Rey died in 1601, but the year of death is left blank on the monument. Perhaps it was already commissioned before he died. An unusual monument of similar date, also in the south aisle, now lost, is known only from records; an elegant classical obelisk to Richard Candish (or Cavendish) an Elizabethan politician and courtier, MP for Denbigh; the long epitaph listing his learning and virtues states that the monument was promised and made by Margaret Countess of Cumberland [fig. 3.10].[16]

3.10 Seventeenth century monument to Richard Candish (Historic England)

39

An active interest in the upkeep of the church is indicated by a document of 1624 recording an exchange of land between George Rey (presumably the son commemorated on the Rey monument) and the Rector, Thomas Westfield.[17] A close called Churchfield was regranted to the rector on condition that the profits therefrom were used for the repair and maintenance of the parish church. Hornsey was not unusual in this respect; recent research on better documented churches around London shows that there were many efforts to keep them in good repair in the early seventeenth century.[18] By this time the interior would have been fitted up with a pulpit for the preacher and seats for the congregation; the pulpit shown in later views of the interior may date from this time [fig. 3.11]. An innovation was a west gallery erected at the charge of Samuel Armitage, Girdler, in 1631, as was recorded on an inscription.[19] The dormer windows shown on later exterior views, which would have provided improved lighting to the nave and west end of the church, may have been added at the same time.

Protestant emphasis was on preaching; the communion service was celebrated only a few times a year at a moveable table. This approach was opposed by William Laud, Bishop of London from 1628 and Archbishop of Canterbury from 1633, who sought to introduce more ceremonial worship, encouraging the adornment of the church building to demonstrate 'the beauty of holiness', and the use of music to enhance the services.[20] Westfield, rector from 1615–37, had a distinguished academic background – he was a Cambridge graduate and an Oxford Doctor of Divinity.[21] Among his other appointments he was a canon of St Paul's and one may assume that he was in sympathy with Laud's approach. Possibly the west gallery at Hornsey was erected for musicians. We have no information about the arrangement of the chancel at this time, but it was likely that changes were made along the lines advocated by Laud, with a railed enclosure for the communion table, set at the east end of the church where the medieval altar had stood. The introduction of such changes, and particularly the new ritual arrangement of the chancel, feared to be a return to Catholic practice, aroused much

3.11 Pulpit (detail from fig. 1.18)

controversy, especially within the City churches, and was one of the principal reasons for Laud's unpopularity and fall in 1640.[22] In 1641–43 there were parliamentary orders for the suppression of Laudian innovations and sweeping changes are recorded to both royal chapels and London parish churches, often creating controversy within individual parishes when parishioners and clergy disagreed. By this time Thomas Westfield had left Hornsey; he was made Bishop of Bristol in 1642 and died two years later.

Thomas Lant was instituted as rector in 1637 by William Juxon (Bishop of London from 1633). After he died in 1688, aged 86, his small stone memorial was placed on the same column as Harrington's [fig. 3.12]. With its coat of arms above a well-carved inscription, it consciously echoes that of his predecessor; indeed as

3.12 Monument to Thomas Lant, Rector, 1686

'Incumbent of this Church 51 yeares' it outdoes Harrington's record not only in age but apparently, in length of service. But the fifty-one years were not a smooth passage. The struggle between King and Bishops on one side, Parliament and Puritans on the other, led to civil war; in 1646 the English episcopacy was abolished by Parliament, and Juxon was deprived of his see and retired to Fulham Palace. Already by 1645 Lant had been brutally 'ejected' from Hornsey Rectory together with his wife and three children. Twenty other Middlesex clergy and ninety-six in London are known to have been deprived of their livings.[23] Remarkably, Parliament was sympathetic about the plight of the destitute clergy families and the Committee for Plundered Ministers agreed that on petition the families should receive a fifth of the revenue. This was ordered for Hornsey in 1645 and repeated in 1647. Where the Lant family lived at this time is unknown. Lant's replacement was a Puritan called Giles Collier, who was followed by S. Winston in 1650, by John Dalton in 1654 and Samuel Bendy in 1658.[24] The last two were appointed by the Wollaston family, who had acquired the Bishop of London's manor of Hornsey. Little is known about this succession of brief incumbencies except that Bendy complained that he received only £92 p.a. and had to pay £16 of this to the Lant family.[25] The Wollastons, it seems, had little interest in Hornsey church; their loyalties lay in Highgate, where Sir John Wollaston founded six almshouses; he died in 1658 and like other Highgate grandees was buried in Highgate Chapel.[26]

3.13 Coffin Plate, Roger Draper 1659

The confusions of the Interregnum are echoed in the earliest surviving register.[27] This is neatly inscribed: 'The Register Book Belonging to the Parish of Hornsey was Bought Anno Dom 1653 by Anthony Black, Abraham Godfrey. Churchwardens', but its contents are erratic and now largely illegible. There are no baptisms recorded between 1656 and 1662, but a large number in the latter year when Lant was back in office, following the Restoration of 1660, which reinstated not only the King but the Anglican church hierarchy.[28] Possibly the Puritan incumbents had disapproved of infant baptism. Burials, however, were recorded throughout the period (around 20 each year), as were marriages, although there seem to have been some irregularities, as an entry for 1675 has three marriages crossed through and a note 'none of these were married by me, Th. Lant'. A relic remaining from this time is a coffin plate to Roger Draper, 1659 [fig. 3. 13]. At some point in the seventeenth century a chest was acquired for the safekeeping of the parish documents. Ironically, the chest has survived, longer than most of the records which it may once have contained.[29]

In 1665 Hornsey was affected by the plague that ravaged London; a special entry in the register gives the names of forty-three people who died at this time, together with a separate list of those who 'dyed of other diseases'. Registers only rarely mention outside events, but there is an exception in 1666: 'Rachel Barnet the daughter of Frances Barnet of the parish of [blank] London was buried the 6th day of September in the same week that the Sitty of London was burnt'. There was also a special collection made on 10 October 1666 'for the solace of those persons' affected by the 'late sad fire in the Sitty of London'. Such a collection was not a unique event; others are recorded in 1667 in response to appeals in aid of other towns further afield which had also suffered fires: Poole in Montgomeryshire, Melcombe Regis, Dorset and Loughborough, Leicestershire.

Bell-ringing was another activity that flourished after the Restoration. Medieval bells had been rung individually for different purposes, such as summoning the faithful to church services and tolling for the dead. From the later sixteenth century the development of the practice of change ringing (ringing the bells in arranged sequences) became popular as a means of marking important events and national festivals expressing loyalty to the Crown.[30] A good peal of bells became a matter of local pride, and was a strong incentive for keeping a church tower in good repair. Tantalising fragments of Hornsey churchwardens' accounts, extant in the earlier twentieth century but not traced since, record payment to the ringers on special occasions – the King's Restoration Day in 1665, the King's Coronation Day in 1674, St George's Day 1675. In the same year they recorded the making of a new bell frame and repairs to the bells.[31] By this date the three pre-Reformation bells listed in 1546 may already have been increased to the 'six tuneable bells' that are recorded in the mid eighteenth century. In the London area in the seventeenth and eighteenth centuries the practice of change ringing was a significant means of developing a sense of community, and in addition to encouraging parish groups of bell-ringers, it became a sport for companies of young men, who toured local churches to demonstrate their skills.[32]

The church furnishings suffered during the Commonwealth period. Thomas Lant is said to have returned to find the parsonage almost entirely ruined and the chancel not much better, which he was obliged to repair at a vast charge.[33] The Puritan incumbents had presumably rearranged the Communion table, and removed any traces of Laudian ceremonies. Gifts made to the church in the later seventeenth century gradually helped to reaffirm the principals of seemly ornament that Laud had promoted. Two flagons, of the first half of the seventeenth century, are mentioned as the gift of Lady Musters, but were probably given after 1662, as the Musters are not recorded in Hornsey before that date.[34] Wine flagons were required to replenish the Communion cup, an indication of a sizeable participating congregation.[35] A cup and paten dating from 1694, also a plate of 1700 given by William Thatcher are also recorded.[36] An elaborately decorated small table of late seventeenth century date, said to be of secular, possibly Dutch origin, may also have been given to St Mary's at this time.[37] Other embellishments of the 1690s, which survived to be noted in the mid eighteenth century, included a pulpit cloth of green plush worked in gold, with the date 1698, and a similar cloth covering the altar.[38]

From 1668 there was a significant gentry family in Hornsey, the Musters, who lived at Brick Place, a house on a moated site north-east of Hornsey village, for nearly forty years.[39] Their most notable contribution to the church was a large

3.14 Monument to Francis Musters, died 1680, when in the church rebuilt in 1833 (British Museum)

wall monument on the north wall, to the east of the pulpit, erected in memory of Sir John Musters' son, Francis, who died in 1680 at the age of sixteen. Its position in the church was characteristic of the way in which chancels continued to be appropriated as burial places for the gentry.[40] The monument was moved to a similar position when the church was rebuilt in 1833 [fig. 3.14]. In recognition of its quality, it is now displayed in the Victoria and Albert Museum. Prohibition of religious images meant that in the seventeenth and eighteenth centuries, funerary figure sculpture provided the principal opportunity in churches for artistic display. The inscription below, now unreadable, but recorded before the monument was dismantled, provides an insight into attitudes of the time.[41]

An architectural surround of columns and pediment frame a portrait of Francis Musters, showing the boy kneeling at prayer at the moment of his death [fig. 3.15]. Cherubs bearing a crown hover above. A realistic skull in the foreground announces his fate.

3.15 Francis Musters monument, detail of upper part (now in Victoria and Albert Museum) attributed to C. G. Cibber

Beside it lies a book inscribed 'The Whole Duty of Man', a popular devotional work first published in 1658. The emphasis on a 'good death', a theme found on other tombs of this period, was made explicit by the verse below.[42]

> *Such was his posture when impartial death*
> *Gave him the summons to resigne his breath*
> *But now his prayers are Hallelujahs grown*
> *Then weep not Reader nor his death bemoan*
> *Why should the living sorrow for the dead*
> *When everlasting glory crowns the head.*

The monument is attributed to the eminent Danish sculptor Caius Gabriel Cibber (1630–1700) who carved the scene of the Fire of London on the Monument in the City, and worked for Wren on St Paul's Cathedral. He gained a high reputation for his ability to express drama and emotion, demonstrated by his sculptures of Melancholy and Madness for Bethlehem Hospital, now in the Museum of London.[43] A precedent for the sensitive treatment of a youthful death is Cibber's more elaborate monument at Withyham, Sussex, commissioned in 1677. It commemorates Thomas Sackville, who died aged thirteen; he lies on a tomb chest, on either side are the expressive kneeling figures of his grieving parents, and on the end of the chest there is a long consolatory verse [fig. 3.16].[44] No documentary evidence is known to connect Cibber with the Hornsey monument, but the similar style of the carving as well as the subject matter provides convincing support for the attribution.

3.16 Monument to Thomas Sackville, Withyham, Sussex, by Caius Cibber, 1677

Other members of the Musters family were commemorated less ostentatiously by ledgers (floor slabs) in the church. The stone to Francis Musters' grandmother, Lady Basset of Tehidy, Cornwall, wife of the royalist supporter Sir Francis Basset, is now in the Garden of Remembrance in the churchyard. It is a fine example of its type, of slate, with bold lettering and an achievement of arms. She died aged 82 in 1682. Her daughter, Sir John Musters' third wife Jane died in 1691; her stone lay in front of the altar rails.[45] The interior views of the old church show other ledger stones laid in the central aisle of the nave [fig 3.17]. Several of these have coats of arms indicating their gentry status, and social hierarchy is further emphasised by the armorial hatchments on the walls These painted boards, popular from the seventeenth century, were made for funerals and retained for display.

The Musters moved away from Hornsey in the early eighteenth century, and there were no more grand memorials, but many lesser ones, witness to the growing fashion among the middle classes for permanent commemoration within the church.

3.17 Hornsey Church, interior looking west by George Arnald, showing ledger stones, lithograph (British Museum)

1. Thyrza Meacock, *A Hundred Year History of St George's Church Hornsey*, Hornsey Historical Society, 2006.
2. William Cole MSS, British Library Add MSS 5836 fo.74ff.
3. W. Norman, *Essex Fonts and Fontcovers*, Baldock, 1986.
4. Royal Commission on Historical Monuments, *East London*, HMSO, 1930, pl. 13.
5. Doreen Agutter, 'Robert Harrington, Parson of Hornsey 1560–1610, a Man of "godly simplicity and singleness of heart"', *Hornsey Historical Society Bulletin* 46, 2005, pp. 1–15.
6. On Grindal see *ODNB*, article 11644.
7. Mill Stevenson, *Monumental Brasses in the British Isles, Appendix 1926-38*, Headley Bros., Ashford and London, 1938.
8. J. Page Phillips, *Palimpsests, the Backs of Brasses*, Monumental Brass Society, 1980, vol. 1, p. 76. After its discovery the brass was mounted in a frame to show both sides. For a brass with comparable details to the palimpsest see the example at Harrow, illustrated in *The Portfolio Plates of the Monumental Brass Society 1894–1984*, Monumental Brass Society, Boydell Press, 1988, fig. 388.
9. H. K. Cameron, 'The Brasses of Middlesex', *Trans. London and Middlesex Archaeol. Soc.* 28, 1977, pp. 309–14.
10. William McBeath Marcham and Frank Marcham, *Court Rolls of the Bishop of London's Manor of Hornsey, 1603–1701*, Grafton, London, 1929, p. 56. The house may have been on the site of The Chestnuts, by Priory Park.
11. The Rey slab is now at St Mary with St George, Cranley Gardens, laid in the floor of the meeting room adjoining the church.
12. Cole MSS, note 2 above.
13. F. A. Greenhill, *Incised Effigial Slabs*, vol. 1, Faber and Faber, London, 1976, p. 875.
14. On London and provincial tombmakers in this period see Nigel Llewellyn, *Funeral Monuments in Post-Reformation England*, Cambridge University Press, 2000, especially ch. 3.
15. Jon Baylis, 'Garrett Hollemans in England', *J. Church Monuments Soc.* 8, 1993, pp. 45–56, note 14.
16. Frederick Teague Cansick, *A Collection of Curious and Interesting Epitaphs Copied from the Existing Monuments of Distinguished and Noted Characters in the Churches and Churchyards of Hornsey ...*, London, 1875, p.5.
17. Marcham and Marcham, *Court Rolls*, p. 61.
18. Valerie Anne Hitchman, *Omnia bene or ruinosa?: The Condition of the Parish Churches in and around London and Westminster c1603–1677*, VDM Verlag, 2009.
19. Cole MSS note 2 above.
20. Graham Parry, *The Arts of the Anglican Counter-Reformation: Glory, Laud and Honour*, Boydell Press, 2006
21. Joseph Foster, *Alumni Oxoniensis 1500-1714*, Parker & Co, Oxford and London, 1891–2, p. 1602.
22. Julie Spraggon, *Puritan Iconoclasm during the English Civil War*, Boydell Press, 2003, ch. 5.
23. The story is told in John Walker's work of Anglican propaganda recounting the sufferings of the clergy, first published in 1714, republished in an abridged version in 1863 by Robert Whitaker, under the shorter title of *The Sufferings of the Clergy of the Church of England during the Grand Rebellion*. For figures of the deprived clergy see A. G. Matthews, *Walker Revised*, Clarendon Press, Oxford, 1948.
24. Matthews, *Walker Revised*, p. 260
25. John H. Lloyd, *The History, Topography and Antiquities of Highgate*, Highgate Literary and Scientific Institution, 1888, p. 94.
26. Ibid., p 132. On Highgate Chapel see Timothy Baker, 'Hermits and Ministers: Highgate Chapel c. 1387-1833', *Hornsey Historical Society Bulletin* 23, 1982, pp. 6–9.
27. LMA: DRO microfilm X001/114.
28. Lant was also made a Canon of St Pauls in 1662; Foster, *Alumni Oxoniensis 1500–1714*, p. 881.
29. Both coffin plate and chest are now at St Mary with St George.
30. David Cressy, *Bonfires and Bells: National Memory and the Protestant Calendar in Elizabethan and Stuart England*, London, 1989.
31. F. W. M. Draper, 'The Hornsey Bells', *Trans. London and Middlesex Archaeol. Soc.* n.s. XI, 1954 p. 120.
32. F. W. M. Draper, 'The Old London Ringing Companies', ibid., p. 27; Peter Clark, *British Clubs and Societies 1580-1800*, Oxford University Press, 2000.
33. Walker's *Ejected clergy*, quoted in Lloyd, History of Highgate, p. 94 (see note 23).
34. Edwin Freshfield, *The Communion Plate of the Parish Churches in the County of Middlesex*, 1897, p. 26, dates the flagons to 1624; RCHME *Middlesex* suggests 1641.
35. Charles Oman, *English Church Plate*, 597-1830, Oxford University Press, 1957.
36. Freshfield, *Communion Plate*, p. 26.
37. Now at St Mary with St George. For its later history see Meacock, *Hundred Year History*, p. 55.
38. Recorded by William Cole in the eighteenth century; see Chapter 4.
39. For numerous references to the Musters see Marcham and Marcham, *Court Rolls*. On Brick Place see VCH *Middlesex*, vol. 6, p. 148; Malcolm Stokes, 'A Moated Site c.1556–1850: Brick or Tower Place and its Owners', *People and Places in Highgate, Hornsey and Wood Green*, ed. J. Schwitzer, 1996, pp. 38–49.
40. The monument was moved from the old church into the building of 1833; and later placed in the north-east porch of the Victorian church. From 1968 it was placed in store, and subsequently acquired by the Victoria and Albert Museum. See further, Chapter 7.
41. The inscription is recorded on photographs of 1968 and by Cansick, *Collection of Curious and Interesting Epitaphs*.
42. For comparable verses expressing the emotions and reactions of bereaved relatives see the collection of inscriptions of 1680–99, in John le Neve, *Monumenta Anglicana*, London, 1718.
43. On Cibber see I. Roscoe, ed., *A Biographical Dictionary of Sculptors in Britain, 1660-1851*, Yale University Press, 2009, p. 274.
44. Rosemary Joekes, 'A Briefe Life: The Memorial to Thomas Sackville', *Country Life*, 19 August 1982, p. 635; C. J. Phillips, *History of the Sackville Family*, vol. 1, London, 1929, p. 420.
45. The position of Jane Musters' ledger was noted by Cole. Cansick recorded the inscription; RCHME (1937) p. 78 noted it lay 'east of the modern church', together with ledgers to Francis Musters, 1682 and to John Barnes junior, 1675. All these have since disappeared.

4.1 Hornsey Church from the south-east, engraving by J. Newton after Samuel Woodburn (1807, British Museum)

CHAPTER 4
The Eighteenth Century

'The parish church is a neat one and not very large, consisting of a square tower at the west end, much too big for the rest of the church, in which hang six tuneable bells, and a clock, which was given to the parish the year preceding, a nave and south aisle, both of which are tiled, the chancel seems to be part of the nave and only distinguished from it by a step up into it and a difference of the arch of the pillars which divides the rest of the nave from the south aisle' [fig. 4.1].

This snapshot of the church in the mid eighteenth century comes from the notes made by the antiquary William Cole, which survive in the British Library.[1] He included a simple sketch of the church seen from the north-east as one approached along the High Road and described both building and contents in some detail. He was examining the church not only for its antiquarian interest but from a practical point of view as he was about to embark on a new step in his career.

William Cole, 1714–1782 [fig. 4.2], was born in Cambridgeshire. After education at Eton and Clare College Cambridge, he inherited some money and spent some years travelling abroad. He was ordained in 1744 and having spent a few years as a curate and private chaplain he was hoping to find a permanent position.[2] In November 1749 he records a visit to the Bishop of London, Thomas Sherlock, at his house in the Temple. After dinner, at around 5 o'clock, Sherlock formally appointed Cole as the new Rector of Hornsey, to fill the vacancy left by Thomas Cartwright who had died earlier that year.

Cole's notes were the result of several visits. His account of the interior suggests that relatively little had changed since the later seventeenth century, but that the church was kept in good order. He records that the altar was 'neatly railed', with paintings of Moses and Aaron flanking texts with the Creed, Lord's Prayer and Ten Commandments – the standard form of adornment which can still be seen in many seventeenth century City Churches [fig. 4.3]. He noted the bricked-up door in the south aisle, which led to the stairs which had provided access to the rood-loft. A 'handsome pulpit of wainscot' stood against the north wall, with the rector's pew opposite. As a good antiquarian he recorded all the inscriptions which revealed past history: the pulpit embellished with 'a cloth of green plush on which is worked in gold 1698' and 'the Altar cloth … of the same stuff'; the 1631 date on the west gallery (see Chapter 3), and another inscription on the south gallery stating that the church had been repaired and beautified in 1714. This is the first known reference to the south gallery. Galleries had developed as a standard solution for extra seating during services where the principal event was a long sermon. The early nineteenth century interior views show the gallery with square front panels similar to those of the pews, possibly all dating from a seventeenth century refitting. The clock [see fig. 1.12] was a more recent novelty, which Cole records had been given by a local benefactor, Daniel Midwinter, 'formerly a bookseller in London but an antient inhabitant of this parish'. The clock cost about £70; and Cole added wisely ' great pity it is that there is not a small fund for

4.2 William Cole in 1768 (engraving published 1805)

4.3 The east end of the church: reredos with texts and figures of Moses and Aaron (from fig. 1.18)

a person to look after it'. Clocks required regular winding. The clock face, erected on the west side of the tower, is visible on Chatelain's drawing of 1760 [see fig. 1.4].[3]

Cole noted with approval that there was also 'a neat vestry on the south side of the tower, in which is a chimney and other conveniences for the rector and officers of the parish to do business in'. This vestry, whose chimney is also visible in the Chatelain view, had been formed from the western bay of the south aisle, adjoining the tower. Together with a window presumably made at the same time, it gave a surprisingly domestic-looking appearance to this corner of the church.

As a dedicated antiquarian and note-taker from an early age (he called his notes his wife and children), Cole was particularly interested in the monuments, giving valuable descriptions of the older monuments mentioned in Chapters 2 and 3. But only half of the seventeen monuments which Cole listed within the church were of some antiquity, the rest were erected in the first half of the eighteenth century, evidence of the fashion for conspicuous memorials among the professional and middle classes. They included a simple tablet to Cole's predecessor, Dr Thomas Cartwright, described as 'an excellent Pastor, a most sincere Friend and the best of Men' [fig. 4.4]. This had been erected on the north wall close to the pulpit by his former curate Samuel Towers. Cole records that on one of his visits to Hornsey Towers asked his permission to carry this out.[4] Cartwright, Cole notes, was buried following his own specifications, '7ft below ground in the north-east corner of his church under another coffin of lead which had to be taken up to make room and afterwards laid on top' – an indication of the shortage of burial space available within the church by this time.

While the condition of the church may have appeared satisfactory, the responsibilities of the rector were less appealing, even though it appears that many tasks were delegated to curates, as was common practice at this period. In the registers

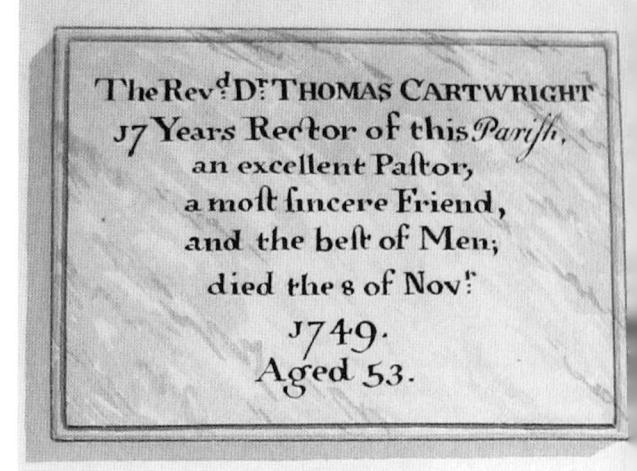

4.4 Wall monuments to John Carter, Goldsmith, 1776; John Reynolds, Surgeon, 1797; Dr. Thomas Cartwright, Rector, 1749. From an aquatint attributed to Thomas Fisher (LMA)

from 1688 onwards Cole found the signatures of five rectors (including himself), one reader, and nine curates. Although the eighteenth century saw a continuous succession of rectors, many of these were not resident in the parish and had other responsibilities. The chapel serving the 'Highgate side' of the parish, with its better-off residents, had its own clergyman. The most eminent of these had been Lewis Atterbury, who settled at Highgate and was appointed preacher at Highgate Chapel in 1695 [fig. 4.5].[5] He was Rector of Hornsey from 1719 until his death in 1731, but his prime loyalty was to Highgate Chapel, and it was there that his monument was erected, although it was moved to Hornsey in 1833. It took the unusual form of a Corinthian column. Only the square base with the inscription now survives [figs. 4.6, 4.7].[6] The Highgate Chapel (on the site of the present chapel of Highgate School) was a substantial building 'as big as its mother church' Cole noted, but had only a small burial ground, inadequate for Highgate's expanding middle-class population. Hornsey had lower burial fees, so the churchyard was the destination for Highgate as well as Hornsey residents.

4.5 Portrait of Lewis Atterbury, Rector (British Museum)

Cole, aware that burials were a significant part of the rectors' duties, made some interesting observations about the churchyard, noting the cold, wet clay soil and 'a Particularity in my churchyard which I never saw anywhere else except tumuli on Gogmagog hills and Salisbury plain …. that is several vaults and Repositories above ground covered with earth to prevent the water covering the body: out of some of which are Troughs or Funnels to let out the water that should happen to come in'. The soggy state of the churchyard does not seem to have discouraged the growing fashion for churchyard memorials, which was gathering pace from the late seventeenth century all over the country. When

4.7 Atterbury monument base (now at St Mary with St George)

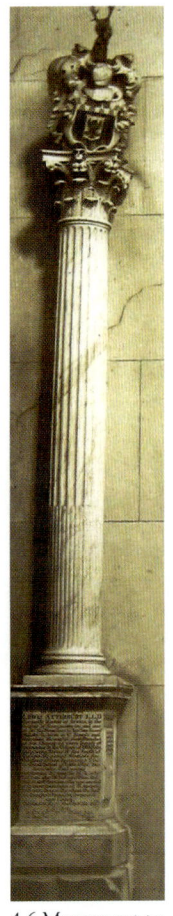

4.6 Monument to Lewis Atterbury photographed before dismantling in 1927 (British Museum)

Cole explored the churchyard, inscriptions on these relatively new monuments were clearly legible: he noted fifteen names, one on a monument on the east wall of the church, and several on what he described as 'altar tombs' (i.e. chest tombs). In the churchyard (which still has some waterlogged areas in winter) there remain a number of chest tombs raised several feet above ground level, generally on brick bases, but only a few of Cole's names can now be linked with surviving monuments [fig. 4.8].[7] Cole took less note of simple headstones; they would have outnumbered the prestigious chest tombs, but have lasted less well. The oldest visible one now remaining in the churchyard is that to Judith Suley, dated 1704, south of the tower [fig. 4.9]. Its present height is misleading; it has sunk into the ground, concealing part of the inscription. Two earlier ones, to Joseph Seaton and Robert Carter, now preserved in the basement of the tower, date from the late seventeenth century [figs. 4.10 and 4.11]. Joseph Seaton's tomb, with its bold, naïve letter spacing, contrasts with the more sophisticated stones with neater lettering and shaped heads that were in fashion by the 1730s. Several of these survive in the area directly north of the tower, and there are others elsewhere in the churchyard [fig. 4.12].

4.8 Raised chest tomb, west border of churchyard

4.9 Tombstone to Judith Suley, 1704

Hornsey was not a popular living; not only were the burial duties onerous, but the income from tithes was fixed at a low level, and the rectory was uninhabitable.[8] Cole records that his predecessor Dr Cartwright had intended to rebuild the rectory but had failed to carry this out before he died in 1749, and had mostly resided in his City parish of St Christopher, Royal Exchange, or stayed with the bishop at Fulham Palace. The rectory, which lay west of the church on the other side of the High Road, was, he reported, 'seated within a mote of running water supplied from the New River'. He investigated the cost of repairs but was told by 'Mr Phillips the King's Surveyor'[9] that he would need to spend £400, and others suggested it would cost even more. Bishop Sherlock had made it clear that he did not want an absentee

4.10 Tombstone to Joseph Seaton, 1693, now in the tower basement

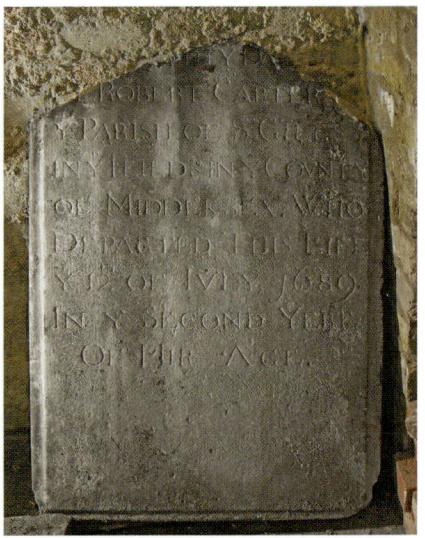

4.11 Tombstone to Robert Carter, 1689, now in the tower basement

4.12 Early to mid eighteenth century tombstones north of the tower

rector and Cole, having discovered that he was expected to repair the rectory, decided in 1751 that he needed to resign, although Sherlock was at first unwilling to accept this. Two years later he was appointed to the Rectory of Bletchley.

Little is known about Cole's immediate successors, John Territt, instituted in 1751, followed by Thomas Lloyd in 1758.[10] The Rectory appears not to have been rebuilt until the 1830s. Meanwhile the day-to-day business of the parish was carried out by the Vestry. A scrappy volume of minutes survives, begun in 1739, which mentions that the Vestry met on some occasions in the parish church, but also in 1749 at the White Lion at Highgate, and also records that in 1750 the Vestry clerk was dismissed and replaced by William Walker.[11] Another book from 1758–68 is largely illegible.[12]

MONUMENTS IN THE CHURCH

The monuments within the church continued to increase, evidence of the area's increasing popularity with middle-class and professional people. Daniel Lysons in his *Environs of London* (1795) describes twenty-eight memorials dating from 1741–89. Although nearly all have disappeared, the appearance of some is recorded in coloured prints made from drawings attributed to Thomas Fisher in the early nineteenth century.[13] One of the most aspirational was that erected by the former curate Samuel Towers to his wife, Hannah, who died in 1753, aged 39. She was the daughter of Edward Halsey, described unflatteringly by Cole as a tradesman residing in Hornsey [figs. 4.13, 4.14]. On the tapered upper part of coloured marble was a coat of arms placed against a tower. The inscription below, recording that she was the only child of 'Edward Halsey Esq, late of this parish' lists her merits at length, adding an encouraging verse for the onlooker, which ends

> *when Virtues such as hers attend on Thee*
> *Fear not to Die, Thoul't be as bles'd as she*

It is typical of the eighteenth century monument designed to inspire virtue by example, while at the same time demonstrating social position and providing a family record. The inscription adds that five of her children were buried nearby, four of them commemorated on a separate tablet (now lost). Her husband Samuel died only a few years later, in 1757, aged forty-five. He had retired young owing to ill health. His epitaph is briefer: 'He was a good Christian, the best of Husbands, the best of Friends'. The phrasing recalls the inscription to Cartwright. Perhaps Towers composed it himself.[14] Other Fisher drawings record less elaborate but dignified wall tablets to a range of middle-class and professional individuals and families, among them Elizabeth Chambers, 1756, and her brother Colonel Edward James, shipwrecked in 1782, [fig. 4.15] and the writer Samuel Buckley, 1741, and his daughter and son-in-law, Elizabeth and Burrage Angier [fig. 4.16]. Early photographs show that many wall tablets were repositioned on the west wall when the church was rebuilt in 1833 [fig. 4.17].

4.13 Monument to Hannah Towers, 1753, aquatint attributed to Thomas Fisher (Bruce Castle Museum)

4.14 The top part of the Hannah Towers monument, now in the tower basement

ALTERATIONS IN THE 1770S

A new phase in the history of the building began in the 1770s. A higher standard of records was set by a well-kept volume of Vestry minutes whose first entry is 26 June 1774, when Thomas Wade was appointed Vestry clerk. It continues to 1782.[15] Initially Henry Poole, curate, signed the Vestry minutes, but in 1775 a new rector, Francis Haultain, was appointed, and on 31 Aug 1775 Poole, described as the 'late curate' handed over the church plate which had been in his custody. The Vestry minutes cover repairs to the church in 1774–75. These were carried out in a very professional manner, including consultation with the public. In April 1775 the inhabitants were asked to assemble in the vestry 'at 4 in the afternoon precisely', in order to inspect the necessary repairs by a bricklayer, plumber, painter and glazier, and a committee was appointed to obtain estimates; the money was to be raised from church rates (hence the need to have agreement from the public). The surveyor employed 'to supervise the workmen's bills' was 'Mr Cowse of Scotland Yard', first mentioned on 8 September 1774. This was the architect Kenton Couse, trained by Henry Flitcroft, 'a competent and conscientious official'[16] who was also Surveyor to the Goldsmith's Company. He is not generally known for his church work, with the interesting exception of Holy Trinity Clapham Common, the church of the Clapham

4.15 Monument to Elizabeth Chambers, 1756 and Col. Edward James, 1782. Aquatint (Bruce Castle Museum)

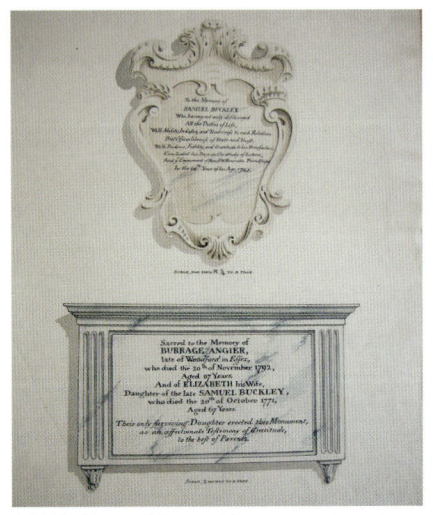

4.16 Buckley and Angier Monuments. Aquatint attributed to Thomas Fisher (Bruce Castle Museum)

4.17 Monuments on the west wall of the nineteenth century church (British Museum)

4.18 The bell frame of 1775 (repositioned in 1833)

Sect, which he designed and built in 1774–76. At Hornsey, a carpenter, William Marshall, was employed for ten weeks at the cost of £72 15s.; a painter, glazier and plumber were employed for the cost of £32 3s. and a bricklayer and plasterer for £33 14s. Other references to improvements – altering the churchwardens' pew and furnishing it with curtain and cushions, and for a new king's arms, cast iron and gilt, suggests a general smartening up of the interior. The emphasis on the churchwardens' pew may indicate that the initiative came from the vestry members rather than from the clergy. Unfortunately it is not clear exactly what else the repair work covered.

Some major work on the tower certainly took place in the 1770s. The minutes record that Mr Marshall was to make a new floor to the clock room in the tower and 'repair the upper floor with such part of the old clock room floor as can be used'. The clock was to be cleansed and put into good repair by a proper person employed for that purpose. There is a reference to new painting and gilding the dial, and to gilding and lettering the vane of the weathervane; both features are visible on artists' views. The puzzle about the work on the tower is the lack of any reference to the bells. But it was at this time that the bells were recast and rehung. The bell frames which survive in the tower bear the date 1775 [fig. 4.18]. The installation of the bulky new frames may explain why it was found necessary to create a new clock floor on the level below the belfry.[17] It is known from later records that the bells were recast by the Chelsea firm of Thomas Jannaway, whose name they carried, together with the date 1775.[18] The lack of any contemporary record of work on the bells could be explained by the existence of a separate fund whose details have been lost.

The third of the Hornsey bells carried a rhyme, also used on other Jannaway bells:

> *The ringers art our grateful notes prolong*
> *Apollo listens and approves our song.*

The pagan classical allusion later earned disapproval among later more strait-laced campanologists. But in the eighteenth century bell-ringing was an accepted secular pastime which coexisted with religious practices, together maintaining the reputation of the parish church as the focus of local society.

As for church services, there was a brief effort at musical improvement. In October 1775 the Vestry minutes record: 'Mr Mihill of Highgate to be allowed a salary of 10 guineas for the ensuing year for instructing such persons who are parishioners of this parish and who may be so inclined to sing in the parish church'. The following month the allowance was cancelled, but in March 1776 the churchwarden was instructed to pay Mr Mihill £2 12s. 6d. (i.e. a quarter of the agreed fee) 'for teaching the parishioners Psalmody'. Congregational singing of metrical versions of the psalms was not a novelty, having been introduced from the late seventeenth century. At Hornsey it seems that a few months of instruction were found to be sufficient. Perhaps the effort reflected the growing awareness at this time of competition from the Methodists.

4.19 Chest tombs to the north of the church. In the foreground is the Morgan family tomb.

The churchyard also featured in the minutes. In 1774 payment for 'weeding and cleansing the Quick' (quickthorn hedge) round the churchyard cost 13s. 4d.; payment for destroying 'foxes, polecats and hedgehogs etc' for two years came to the sum of £2 14s., (while the churchwardens' dinner cost £2). An 'Umbrellow' (perhaps for use at funerals), cost 12s. These were only a part of the vestry's concerns; their activities with regard to highways, poor relief and the rebuilding of the poorhouse lie outside the scope of this study, but show a lively concern with the good ordering of the parish.[19]

Less is known about the 1780s. In 1780 Charles Shepherd was appointed Rector.[20] He held the post for forty-nine years but took little interest in local affairs, spending most of his time at

4.20 Chest tombs (mostly dismantled) on the south side

another living in Northamptonshire. The Vestry's letters of complaint to him about the unsatisfactory character of the occasional curates he employed, and his prevaricating replies, reveal an unhappy situation in the 1790s.[21] By this time, interest in Hornsey Church as a picturesque antiquarian relic (see Chapter 1) coincided with growing dissatisfaction with the capacity of the building. The surrounding countryside was becoming populated with an increasing number of middle-class villas, but both seats in the church and space for burial in the churchyard were inadequate. In 1792 the sexton reported that there was no space to dig further graves without disturbing recent ones. On 6 November 1794 a special Vestry meeting reported that the Church was 'under great decay and becoming dangerous'. A new gallery had been proposed but would not be satisfactory, what was needed was the complete repair of the church, the addition of a north aisle and the enlargement of the churchyard. A committee was set up, but the scheme was abandoned at a meeting on 3 April 1795 because of the 'very great expense' and the 'very many unforeseen difficulties'. A more modest proposal just to enlarge the churchyard by purchasing one rood and 20 perches from the rector was considered on 18 December 1799. In February 1800 borrowing a sum of money for purchasing part of the glebe land to extend the churchyard was discussed but rejected. But the comfort of the clergyman officiating at funerals was considered and in 1807 it was resolved to provide 'a box for the minister to stand in at the funerals in the churchyard in wet weather'.

CHURCH AND CHURCHYARD AT THE START OF THE NINETEENTH CENTURY

The churchyard continued to fill with tombs, with new headstones squeezed in among the older ones. From later plans it appears that a pattern was emerging of a row of large chest tombs on either side of the church. On the north side three such tombs still remain standing [fig. 4.19]; on the south only one remains but the relics of others can be seen [fig. 4.20].[22] From the end of the eighteenth century headstones of sandstone began to appear, imported from the Midlands (now connected to London by canal routes), as an alternative to the Portland stone used previously. In contrast to weathered limestone faces, crisply cut lettering showed up well against a smooth sandstone surface [fig. 4.21]. Sandstone slabs, however, are vulnerable to frost and pollution, as can be seen in the case of the Ware family tomb, where the inscription is on a large low horizontal slab, a type of monument that was a popular alternative to chest tombs in the early nineteenth century [fig. 4.22]. This is one of a large number of tombs crammed into the north-east area of the churchyard. It is possibly that this area furthest from the church may have been developed in the early years of the nineteenth century, incorporating some waste land beside the High Road, as pressure for space became increasingly intense [see fig. 1.2, p. 10].

4.21 Sandstone headstone to Henry Pott, 1816

4.22 Ware family tomb, early nineteenth century, with delaminating inscription

Meanwhile there were minor improvements to the building. The church windows were replaced, probably after 1800, although no record survives of this work. The irregular medieval Gothic windows visible in the views up to the 1790s gave way to large round-arched openings filled with small panes of plain glass. The interior was enhanced by some private gifts.[23] An organ was installed on the west gallery as a result of a legacy of 1806 from John William Paul [fig. 4.23]. Four extra pews in the gallery were added at the expense of William Samuel Towers (very likely a descendant of the mid eighteenth century curate). Towers was clearly a significant donor who required recognition. In 1809 it was recorded that his gift of new velvet hangings, hassocks and a carpet in the chancel should be inserted on the Board of Benefactors (not a usual type of entry on such boards). New monuments in the church continued to be added. An unusual one reflects the social hierarchy of the time, a simple memorial to two servants: Mary Parsons 'the diligent, faithful and affectionate servant of one Family' and her 'Friend and Companion' Elizabeth Dicker, the former dying in 1806, the latter in 1809. Domestic servants were rarely honoured by memorials within the church. Was the stone put up by the unknown family whom they served, for 57 and 47 years respectively?[24]

The need for more seating continued to be pressing; in 1815 enlargement of the gallery was again proposed (simpler than building a new aisle) and was grudgingly agreed provided the cost did not exceed £90. Raising the church rates for such a purpose was not popular and it is not clear whether it was carried out; in 1825 some additional seats were approved, provided that the cost was met by private subscription. But the time of piecemeal improvements was drawing to an end; a few years later a more radical approach would be adopted.

4.23 Organ on the west gallery in the early nineteenth century (detail from fig. 3.17)

---

[1] William Cole MSS, British LIbrary Add MSS 5836 f.74ff.

[2] *ODNB*, article 5863.

[3] Midwinter also left money to the Stationers' Company to pay the costs of apprentices from Hornsey. Lloyd, *The History, Topography and Antiquities of Highgate*, Highgate Literary and Scientific Institution, 1888, p.107.

[4] The Cartwright memorial is now in the garden behind St Mary with St George.

[5] Atterbury was well known from his published sermons and held several other positions, including Chaplain to Queen Anne, and Rector of Shepperton from 1707 until his death in 1731. See *ODNB*, article 873.

[6] The base, now at St Mary with St George, Cranley Gardens, records Atterbury's career and mentions his children and his grand-daughter, Penelope Sweetapple.

[7] Examples are the Morgan family tomb, to which Cole gives the date 1716, describing it as 'brick and marble, in the north east corner', and the ' Smith children', which can be identified as a large chest tomb in the west border close to the tower.

[8] Cole reported that the tithes were fixed at 4d. per acre throughout the parish, with 40 acres of glebe land let for £60.

[9] Possibly Joseph Phillips, a royal clerk of the works who was dismissed from his post at the Royal Mews in 1746. H. M. Colvin et al., *History of the King's Works*, vol. V, London, 1976, p. 104.

[10] Lloyd, *History of Highgate*, p. 89.

[11] LMA DRO 20/C1/1.

[12] LMA DRO 20/C1/2.

[13] For Fisher's drawings see chapter 1, note 18.

[14] The Towers monument was moved to the new building in 1833, placed on the west wall of the nave, and thus left exposed to the elements and vandalism after the body of the church was demolished in 1927 (see fig. 7.6). The upper part of the monument survives, much battered, and is now in the basement of the tower.

[15] LMA DRO 20/C1/3.

[16] H. M. Colvin, *A Biographical Dictionary of British Architects 1600-1840*, Yale University Press, 1995, pp. 274–5.

[17] It is unclear exactly how these levels worked as in 1833 this level of the tower was largely rebuilt, and the bell-frame raised to a higher level. After 1833 the upper levels consisted of the bell-ringing chamber, the clock floor and a much taller belfry with the bells.

[18] On Jannaway see H. B. Walters, 'London Church Bells and Bellfounders', *Trans. St Paul's Ecclesiological Soc.* VI, 1907, p. 115, and H. B. Walters, Church Bells of England, Oxford University Press, 1912, p. 219.

[19] See further: Richard Samways, 'Local Democrats: The Hornsey Vestry in Action c.1740-1800', *Hornsey Historical Society Bulletin 28*, 1987, pp. 26–34.

[20] According to Lloyd in *History of Highgate*, Haultain died in 1780, but a Francis Haultain is recorded as holding posts at East Ham and later at Elstree and Weybridge. See J. Foster, *Alumni Oxoniensis*, Parker & Co, Oxford and London, 1888.

[21] Samways, 'Local Democrats'.

[22] The remaining raised chest tomb on the south side, to the Mitchell family, now has the curious features of a slab placed out of sight on top, with a long inscription recording family members with dates of death from 1796–1842. There was also an interior memorial recording the names, later moved to the Victorian church.

[23] Vestry minute book DRO 20/C1/4 1803–1834.

[24] This marble slab, recorded by Cansick as in the church, was removed at an unknown date (possibly when the building was demolished in 1927), and was discovered in a Muswell Hill back garden.

5.1 Hornsey village from the north, drawing (Bruce Castle Museum)

CHAPTER 5

The Early Nineteenth Century: The Rebuilding

Despite the growing population, in the early years of the new century Hornsey was still a village with a recognisably ancient parish church, a picturesque landmark celebrated by prints and a collector's token (see Chapter 1). Hornsey's rustic character offered a respite from the urban expansion creeping north through Islington and Hackney [fig. 5.1]. The rural appeal of the village was cherished not only by explorers of the London environs but by the local residents, as can be seen in the concern of the Vestry to maintain standards. In 1826 the minutes record that dumping of waste timber had 'endangered the beauty of the village'. Steps were taken to restore the 'delightful village to its original beauty' by clearing the offending area, laying grass and erecting railings to prevent similar nuisances in future.[1] Antiquarian appreciation of the church was sharpened when the proposals for its rebuilding were revived, culminating in the perceptive account in *The Gentleman's Magazine* of 1832 written by E. J. Carlos very shortly before demolition took place.[2] There was particular concern about the need to record the appearance of the monuments; several drawings of the George Rey slab were made (including one by Carlos himself),[3] and the artist Thomas Fisher was employed in making records of others. George Arnald's lithographs capture the rustic atmosphere of both setting and interior at this time (see

Chapter 1). But not all responded to the charm. 'The old church was very plain and the service very drowsy', Henry Bachelor (born 1823) recalled in his old age.[4] He recalled the whitewashed walls, the congregation sitting in high straight-backed pews of unpainted deal, the children squeezed into the organ gallery at the west end, distracted by the bees trapped around the dormer window above. Bee stings were treated with the oil used to reduce the squeaking of the organ. According to Bachelor, it was a barrel organ, which the schoolmaster wound by hand, with a repertoire limited to a few traditional hymns.

Thirty years earlier, in the midst of the Napoleonic wars, suggestions for rebuilding the church had come to nothing. The situation in the 1820s was very different. The introduction of the national census in 1801 had focused public attention on the changing character of the expanding British population. Not only was there was a lack of Anglican churches in the fast-growing industrial areas in the Midlands and the north, but seating capacity in existing churches in and around London and other older cities could not cope with demand. Hornsey's growing middle-class population felt the need for a respectable church where families could mark their status by renting their own pews.

Previously efforts to improve matters had been hampered by cumbersome regulations about building new churches, and inadequate funds available to assist existing ones. A group of energetic Anglican lay churchmen campaigned for change, galvanised by awareness of the growing strength of Methodism as an alternative, and by fears that lack of religious instruction could encourage public unrest and rebellion. The Church Building Society was founded in 1818, with the object of collecting donations to support grants to assist individual churches and in the same year a parliamentary Act granted one million pounds for the construction of new churches in areas of need. Already by 1821, 85 new churches had been built; by 1830 the suburbs north of the City were served by eight built with parliamentary money, and numerous existing churches in Middlesex (and elsewhere) had been given grants by the Church Building Society, from 1828 named the Incorporated Church Building Society (ICBS), which funded enlargements, reseating and additional galleries. Both the Commission set up by the Act and the ICBS imposed strict standards of building, so there was a fund of experience to draw on, as well as some lively debate as to whether Gothic or Classical was the best style to choose, for economic as well as aesthetic reasons.[5]

To achieve change at Hornsey, which prided itself on its traditional village character, growing public interest in church building, and even the possibility of a grant, were not enough. Leadership was needed, and this was provided when a new rector was appointed in 1829. The Vestry minutes for 22 September conclude with a formal note 'thanking the Revd. Richard Harvey our worthy Rector who the parishioners have for the first time met this day' [fig. 5.2].

Harvey was appointed by the new bishop of London, Charles Blomfield, following the death of the previous incumbent, the largely absentee Charles Shepherd. Harvey was then aged thirty. He had previously been a curate at Hackney, where he would have come into contact with leading members of the campaigning High Church group known as the 'Hackney Phalanx'. The rector of Hackney, John James Watson, was the brother of the highly influential Joshua Watson, commissioner of the 1818 Act and active administrator

5. THE EARLY NINETEENTH CENTURY

of many church charities. Harvey's next post was as curate at St Botolph Bishopsgate where Blomfield was rector in 1820–24, until he became Bishop of Chester, returning to London as its bishop in 1828. Harvey's longstanding friendship with Blomfield was signified by the fact that he was a pall-bearer at Blomfield's funeral in 1857.[6]

Blomfield was a firm believer in the need for new churches, becoming a member of the Church Building Commission in 1825. As Bishop of London he set up the Metropolitan Building Fund in 1835 and a special fund four years later for new churches in the impoverished area of Bethnal Green.[7] By the time of his death in 1857, 200 new churches had been built in his diocese (which then covered Essex and much of Hertfordshire as well as Middlesex). Harvey was to follow his example, establishing new churches as the older settlements within the old parish of Hornsey expanded. But first something had to be done about the inadequacy of the parish church and its churchyard.

5.2 Portrait of Richard Harvey, Rector. Lithograph by G.F. Sintzenich (LMA)

Henry Bachelor recalled the churchyard as little cared for, overseen by a sexton who was 'a half-witted but exceedingly obscene old fellow'; it was a playground for local youth, and the young Henry and his friends delighted in exploring the 'bone hole', the former stairs to the rood loft; he notes there was a door to it inside the church, but it was only accessible from outside. 'Slim little fellows like I was squeezed through the arrow-slit and jumped down onto the bones', handing them out for pitched battles and breaking them to pieces on the tombstones.[8] His account reflects the typically overcrowded state of churchyards; new graves inevitably disturbed older ones; the disused old stair turret had become a handy repository for what was dug up.

Steps to enlarge the churchyard were already in progress in 1829. In April, Mr Prickett, a local surveyor, was appointed to value land for a proposed addition. Two roods and two perches[9] were estimated at £77. The Vestry agreed to apply to the Bishop for consecration of the land, but it was some years before it came into use. Plans for the church must have

63

been in active consideration over the next two years, for by May 1831 the Vestry had reached a decision. At the vestry meeting on 23 May with 38 people present, 'for purpose of taking into consideration the serious inconvenience the inhabitants of this parish are put to for want of sittings in the church, with a view to adopt such plan for enlargement of the same as may be deemed necessary', it was resolved that 'churchwardens agree with George Smith of the Old Jewry, surveyor, to prepare a plan and estimates... not exceeding £50... for rebuilding the body of the church to contain 900–1000 sittings and report generally on the capability of the present building to be extended or repaired'. A building committee with eleven members was set up under the curate, Richard Haygarth, but it is clear that it was Harvey who was the driving force; a note adds that the thanks of the meeting were to be given to the rector for bringing the matter before the Vestry.[10]

The choice of the architect George Smith (1782–1869) displays some independence from the activities of both the Church Building Commission and the Church Building Society, for he was not among the architects associated with either group. But Smith had a solid reputation in the City of London as a surveyor, in particular through his work for the wealthy Mercers' Company.[11] As Surveyor to the City's southern district he had been responsible for the rebuilding of the tower and east front of the City's baroque Royal Exchange, demonstrating his versatility and ability to handle complicated tasks, and his work would have been familiar locally, as he was architect of the Mercers' Whittington Almshouses on Highgate Hill, completed in 1822. Also, significantly, in 1828–32 he was engaged in building a church, St Michael Blackheath on the Cator estate, for which he acted as Surveyor [fig. 5.3]. Like many architects at this period, he was able to work in a variety of styles, depending on the commission. Both the Whittington Almshouses [fig. 5.4] and St Michael demonstrate his interest in a spare Gothic style, and it was this that he proposed for Hornsey. We do not know whether his clients' views played a part in the choice, but in the 1830s Gothic was winning over Classical as a choice of style for new churches, particularly for those in a rural setting, exploiting the association of Gothic with religious feeling that had already been fostered in the later eighteenth century by the Romantic movement.[12]

The brisk progress over the next two years can be followed in detail from the Vestry minutes and correspondence.[13] Smith's

5.3 St Michael Blackheath, architect George Smith

5.4 Whittington Almshouses, architect George Smith (Guildhall Collection, LMA)

estimates were submitted in June 1831: the estimate for rebuilding the body of the church was £4,594 for 902 sittings. Enlargement, providing 280 additional sittings, would cost £4,919, (including new heating). The existing church had seats for 400, of which 180 were free seats, mostly inconvenient benches for children in the gallery. Not surprisingly, rebuilding was preferred, provided extra money could be raised from the ICBS; the Vestry hoped for an additional £3,000. Fundraising began, and by 25 July house-to-house appeals had produced £1,856, with donations ranging from £100 to a penny ha'penny.

By November the total funds raised from the appeal had risen to £2,009 0s. 6d., of which £1,912 0s. 6d. had already been collected and 'deposited in the Bank of England', as Harvey explained in the grant application submitted to the ICBS. His accompanying letter explained the complicated position in Hornsey. He stated that although the parish population in 1831 was 4,856,[14] only 2,286 lived in 'Hornsey side'; the 'Highgate side' inhabitants had already subscribed to a new church to replace the old Highgate chapel (St Michael, South Grove, designed by Lewis Vulliamy, begun in 1830), for which they were also about to pay pew rent. They would therefore not be prepared to contribute to a new church in Hornsey, from which they would not benefit. The ICBS imposed strict conditions on its applicants, among them the demand that there should be a proportion of free seating (like the Church Building Commission, it accepted reluctantly that pew rents were an unfortunate financial necessity to support the clergy). The plans submitted by George Smith [figs. 5.5, 5.6] showed that a total of 960 seats could be provided, 560 more than in the present building, and that 300 of these would be free. As was customary, the free seats would be of smaller dimensions, 18 by 30 inches instead of 20 by 36. The ICBS was satisfied, but granted only £700, less than was hoped for.[15] Harvey had to work hard to persuade the Vestry, with its majority of Highgate members, to agree to raise a rate of £1,500 to cover the gap, but this was agreed in January 1832.

Smith's plans followed the common pattern of new churches of this time: a compact, aisled church with a gallery on each side reached by stairs within north and south entrance porches. The interior was to be well lit by clerestorey windows as well as aisle windows. A small projecting sanctuary housed the altar. The plan shows a freestanding central pulpit prominently sited in front of the altar, visible from every side, emphasising the significance of

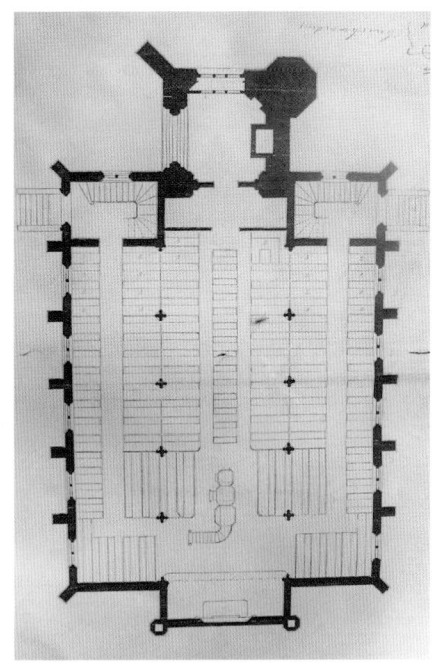

5.5 Ground plan of Smith's proposed church, 1832 (Incorporated Church Building Society, Lambeth Palace Library)

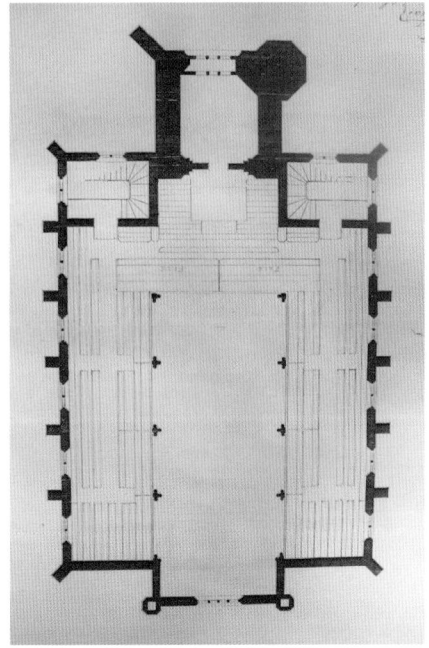

5.6 Gallery plan of Smith's church, 1832 (Incorporated Church Building Society, Lambeth Palace Library)

the preacher. Seats were squeezed into every corner on two levels, including the west gallery which abutted the tower. Those in the west gallery and in the four back rows on the ground floor were marked as 'Free'. The plan also shows temporary seats down the central aisle, but even with these it is difficult to imagine how 300 people of modest dimensions could be accommodated on the free seats. A total provision of around 1000 seats was the standard set by the Commission in the 1820s, with one fifth of them free. The hoped-for provision of free seats at Hornsey was a higher proportion of the total, but may have been over-optimistic.

With the final funds still awaiting collection, tenders were invited in January 1832 and in March, the cheapest, from Piper & Son, at £5,250, was accepted. The committee chose the modern method of employing a contractor rather than making separate agreements with different trades. Thomas Piper & Son was a well-established City firm for three generations. Thomas Piper II, described as 'a man of active benevolence', had worked on several major buildings in the 1820s–30s including the London Customs House and Goldsmiths' Hall, as well as the steeple of the City church of St Antholin, and so would have been well known to George Smith.[16]

BURIAL VAULTS

In order to provide the additional funding needed, an ingeniously pragmatic solution was adopted, agreed at the same time as the tenders: the sale of burial vaults beneath the church. The price was 40 guineas (£42) each, in return for remission of the burial fee. It was urged that building the church above vaults would also make the church dryer and warmer, a plausible argument given the damp record of the churchyard. Burial crypts below churches had a long tradition, and many of the urban churches built in the eighteenth century, such as the great East London churches by Hawksmoor, were provided with crypts for this purpose. Some of the new churches of the early nineteenth century followed the practice, for example the new St Pancras on Euston Road (1821), where a sober prominence was given to the doors to the crypt in the grand Grecian side porches.

No such magnificence was proposed at Hornsey: the plan was adapted to include external crypt entrances contrived discreetly at the east end beside the sanctuary. However, Hornsey was at the very end of this tradition. From the 1830s the whole practice of burial within and around urban churches was coming under scrutiny. The scandal of the unhealthy state of overcrowded city churchyards led to the establishment of more spacious private and municipal cemeteries on the urban fringes, and in 1854 burial below the church was forbidden by an Order in Council.[17] The Hornsey vaults were in use for only twelve years, the last burial taking place in 1843. A plan attached to the faculty of 1832 gives the names of those who had subscribed, showing that the vaults were arranged as twelve 'catacombs' below the north and south sides, each able to contain eight coffins [fig. 5.7]. The select list includes several names which appear frequently in the Vestry minutes: Henry Warner of The Priory (the principal local landowner), George Buckton and Charles Rogers were all on the building committee and no doubt felt it appropriate to set an example; John Bumpstead, plumber of Crouch End, was churchwarden in 1833 and, with Thomas Sadleir, upholsterer of Highgate, was a Guardian of the Poor in 1838.

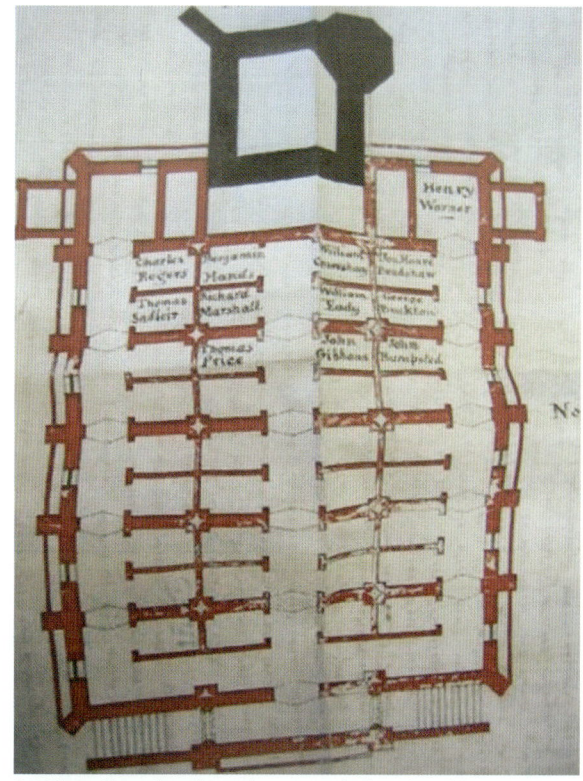

5.7 Plan of burial vaults with names of subscribers (St Mary's Hornsey, LMA DR020/B2/3)

It is convenient to mention here, in advance of the discussion of the rest of the building, that a few remnants of the crypt survived the demolition of the church in 1927. The brick west walls that still abut the tower include examples of the circular iron ventilator grills at crypt level which provided some light to the interior [fig. 5.8]. Those along the south side of the church can be seen clearly on old photos and drawings. For unknown reasons, when the building was demolished in 1927, one of the vaults was not filled in. An empty brick-lined chamber, corresponding to the vault assigned to Henry Warner on the plan, remains beneath two large stone slabs within the Garden of Remembrance, north-east of the tower.

5.8 West wall with crypt ventilator

THE REBUILDING OF THE CHURCH, 1832-33

An anonymous watercolour dated 22 May 1832 shows the old church being stripped out [fig. 5.9]. The south gallery front has been taken down leaving only the floor in place, timbers and broken panelling lie around, a darker patch on the east wall indicates where something has been removed. Another watercolour shows the exterior, with the medieval roof, which had remained hidden above the plaster ceiling, in course of demolition [fig. 5.10]. Only after work had started was another change proposed. The original plans had assumed that the old tower would be retained. Now it was realised that it would appear seriously out of scale with the new building. The matter came before the Vestry in September, when the building committee reported that it would be 'desirable to increase the elevation of the tower'. 'By their directions a plan and estimate had been prepared which including the necessary alterations of the Bells amounted to about £300'. This was agreed and the money was to be raised by a loan. We do not know whether the architect or the committee provided the impetus for this. Smith certainly had an interest in towers, as one can see from his remarkably original one at St Michael Blackheath. But one can sense the enthusiasm of the building committee as well. At the Vestry meeting of 28 March 1833, only six months later, the committee reported 'with much satisfaction to the Improvement effected by raising the tower which they are of the opinion has been accomplished in a manner highly creditable to the architect and builders' [fig. 5.11]. Other progress was reported. A loan of £2,000 had been obtained from a single (unnamed) donor, at a rate of 4.5 per cent. The catacombs had been completed and would cause no further disturbance; a hot water heating system was recommended, the carriageway to the church on the north side was to be extended to provide access to the entrance to the vaults. This Vestry meeting was held at the workhouse, as the old vestry no longer existed and the new vestry which was to be made in the tower was not yet ready.

5.9 The east end of the old church. Demolition in progress, 1832, watercolour (Museum of London)

Surviving records include both the detailed specifications for building the church and for the alterations to the tower.[18] The foundations were to be of concrete, three feet in depth and two feet wider than the walls to be erected on them; the mortar mix for the brickwork was specified.[19] Drainage was to be achieved by a cesspool 20 feet in depth and 10 feet in diameter, brick lined, domed over, with a stone with a handle for lifting (no trace of this has been found). It is interesting to note that cast iron was to be used for columns and beams, with wrought iron straps, and the nave and aisles ceilings were to be of plaster, with moulded ribs, all to be painted in imitation of stone. As was common practice at this time, the Gothic style was achieved through surface detail applied to modern materials, without any attempt at medieval methods of construction.

The original instructions for the alterations to the tower indicate a thorough restoration was intended. They specified taking down the walls to the level of the 'lead Flatt' (i.e. the flat roof) and rebuilding them using such old material as was approved; cutting out bulged and defective work in other parts of the tower; inserting new belfry windows with frames of Bath

5.10 Demolition of St Mary Hornsey, 1832, watercolour (Museum of London)

5.11 The completed church 1836, from the south, drawing (Bruce Castle Museum)

stone, also cornices, water tables, embrasures and battlements of Bath stone, as shown on the drawings. The turret staircase was to be continued up to the lead flat with York stone steps and newels, and at the bottom was to have new steps of Portland stone; the tower was to have Portland stone quoin stones (corner stones) properly worked, and a Portland stone door-case with Gothic head at the top of the turret stair leading to the flat. There was to be a Gothic Portland stone chimneypiece in the vestry. This, it seems, was intended to be on the level of the lowered ground floor, which was to be excavated to a depth of two feet, as there is a reference to two doorways in the 'vestry' (the doorway to the turret stair and the new doorway to the exterior). On the floor above two openings (i.e. the south and east arches) were to be bricked up, and the external wall (i.e. the wall blocking the arch which formerly led into the south aisle) was to be faced with stone taken from the present building. The west window was to be reglazed, and the interior walls were to be rendered, 'jointed and coloured to imitate stone'. The ringing loft, at the next level, was to be lined with matchboarding to a height of 4 feet, the ceiling repaired, and a door inserted to the organ gallery; the clock floor was also to be repaired.

5.12 A view of the clock level above the ringing chamber; south wall with sixteenth century brickwork retained

5.13 Tower, west side, with window in ringing chamber, repositioned clock and new belfry

So much for the specification. But as both the accounts and the existing building reveal, there were a number of divergences from the instructions. Building work was completed in 1833 and the church was consecrated on 24 July, although work was still in progress on the tower. The accounts were not presented until 1835. They came to a total of £7,484 5s. 1d., considerably more than the agreed contract cost of £5,240, and so required justification and discussion of the £1,077 5s. 1d. spent on 'extras'. The heightening of the tower, a late instruction, had at first been estimated as costing an extra £300. But the restoration work had proved more extensive than anticipated; the 'defective state of the old wall required taking down and rebuilding much lower than originally intended', while no provision had originally been made for the vestry room. Other extras were enumerated. Work on the bells had been contracted out to the specialist firm of Mears (Thomas Mears of the Whitechapel Bell Foundry) and had cost £93 15s. 9d., involving scaffolding and lowering and raising the bells. The rebuilding and raising of the belfry level of the tower had involved bricklayers, masons, carpenters and labourers over several weeks. Moving the bells had involved other work, including the creation of a 'circular kerb' in the ceiling to allow for the passage of the bells. This took the carpenters three days, and they spent another five days on the clock. The heightening of the tower had made it possible to raise the clock-face on the west face to a higher level (there is no reference to the second clock-face on the north side, which was added later). Two windows were created in the ringing loft [fig. 5.13]. Other costs included the 'unavoidable' one of fixing the 'warm water apparatus', various improvements to the interior of the church made at the discretion of the architect, and the erection of entrance gates which 'afford great public accommodation and occasion general satisfaction to those who have been the principal subscribers in aid of the undertaking'. The cost of the gates was £58 13s. Raising the additional funds to pay for the extra costs was achieved largely through individual donations: an additional £50 from the Bishop (who had already given £100), £50 from the Rector, £100 each from George and Henry Warner, and smaller sums from others. The cost of completing the 'catacombs', £425, had been covered by the individual subscriptions. Agreements over the final costs and the fees payable to the clerk of the works and the architect were finally reached on 19 August 1835 and were printed as a separate document.[20]

THE TOWER

The tower in its present form still reveals many aspects of the work undertaken in 1833–34. Despite the heightening, the first impression of the exterior is of a building older than the 1830s, because rough rubble stone is used throughout for the walling, the upper part making use of

5.14 Tower, south side with new basement entrance; the wall above is faced with reused stone blocking the medieval arch

dark stone, no doubt from the old building, interspersed with lighter material [fig. 5.14]. The dressed stone is of many types and dates; on the outside, some of the white Portland stone used to repair the quoins and buttresses may predate the 1830s. Smith, it seems, tried to avoid radical rebuilding; the worn stones of the internal arches on east and south sides were only partly replaced; the west window was repaired, but, judging from the old views, on a like-for-like basis. The ringing chamber was given small windows to south and west and the clockface moved to the floor above. The entirely new belfry, to which the old bell-frame was moved, was lit by tall two-light windows on each face, a contrast to the squat straight-headed belfry windows of the medieval building. They have Gothic tracery, matching the windows of the new church, but with openings filled by a lattice pattern of shields in quatrefoils, which appears to be made of some kind of cast stone [fig 5.15]. Tall belfry windows of comparable proportions were a feature of many new churches of the 1820s–30s, giving dignity to towers that many considered were the essential distinguishing mark of Anglican churches.[21] The design of Hornsey's top level with its new battlements and upstanding turret is however a deliberate tribute to the late medieval tradition of the Middlesex area (see Chapter 2), but with a curious addition. At the corners of the tower and on the turret are some very worn pieces of sculpture [figs. 5.16 and 17]. Their grotesque heads give them the appearance of gargoyles, although they do not serve any drainage function, as this is achieved by a drainpipe on the north wall. There are worn heads also at the ends of the dripstone above the reset clock [fig. 5.20]. Neither the views of the old church nor the antiquarian descriptions acknowledge these carvings, and there is no reference to them in the

5.15 Detail of belfry window with cast stone tracery

5.16 'Gargoyles' below the parapet

5.17 'Gargoyle', detail

5.18 Interior of the ringing chamber

accounts; they must have been introduced by Smith and Piper & Son to reinforce the impression of antiquity deliberately created by the reuse of stonework from the old church. Pipers executed much architectural stonework in the City of London; acquiring such fragments would not have been difficult.

Inside, the most drastic change was the creation of a basement, with its own entrance on the north side, and insertion of a floor to tally with the level of the new church raised above the burial crypt. At some point (probably after the inclusion of the burial crypt required the change in levels) it was decided to adapt the well-lit upper storey (on the same level as the church) as the vestry room, rather than site it at ground level as first proposed. A fireplace was made at this upper level, connecting to the existing flue, but there is no evidence now for any Portland stone fireplace surround. Portland stone does not seem to have been used (although originally specified) for the doorways in the basement and at the top of the turret, and the basement fireplace remained unaltered. Above the vestry, the walls of the bell-ringing chamber were boarded; the full-height boarding which still exists presumably dates from this time [fig. 5.18]. The east face of the wall (now external) shows no evidence for the proposed opening to the organ gallery. This level of the tower was entirely separate from the church, and could

5.19 Turret, interior brickwork, showing the transition from sixteenth-century to nineteenth-century work

only be accessed from the basement. This may have been seen as an advantage; it was often considered preferable to give potentially rowdy bell-ringers their own entrance. The most obvious contrast between old and new is inside the turret; above the level of the ringing chamber the steps change to thinner slabs of York stone, and yellow stock brick replaces red brick for the internal walls [fig. 5.19].

5.20 Clock dripstone with reused carved head

[1] St Mary Hornsey Vestry minutes LMA DRO 20/C1/4.

[2] *The Gentleman's Magazine*, vol. 102, pt. 2, 1832, pp. 11–14. See also Chapter 1.

[3] BL Carlos notebooks: Drawing by Edward John Carlos of George Rey tomb in Hornsey church, BL Add MSS 25706.

[4] Peter Barber, ed., *Gin and Hell-Fire: Henry Batchelor's Memoirs of a Working-class Childhood in Crouch End 1823–1837*, Hornsey Historical Society, 2004, p. 27.

[5] M. H. Port, *Six Hundred New Churches: The Church Building Commission 1818-1856*, London, 1961, rev. edn. 2006.

[6] Malcolm Johnson, *Bustling Intermeddler? The Life and Work of Charles James Blomfield*, Gracewing, 2001, p. 149.

[7] Johnson *Bustling Intermeddler? op. cit.*, ch. 7.

[8] Barber, *Gin and Hell Fire*, p. 44.

[9] A rood is one quarter of an acre or one tenth of a hectare; a perch is one fortieth of a rood.

[10] Building committee members listed in 1831 were: the Revd. Richard Haygarth, Mr Buckton, Mr H. Warner, Mr Rogers, Mr Lucas, Mr Viney, Mr Sadleir, Mr Worley, Mr Groves, Mr Townshend, Mr Geo. Prickett, Mr Bage.

[11] H. M. Colvin, *A Biographical Dictionary of British Architects, 1600–1840*, Yale University Press, 1995, pp. 890–2.

[12] S. Bradley, 'The Roots of Ecclesiology. Late Hanoverian attitudes to Medieval Churches', '*A church as it should be*': *The Cambridge Camden Society and its Influence*, ed. Christopher Webster and John Elliott, Shaun Tyas, 2000, pp. 22–44.

[13] LMA DRO 20/C1/4.

[14] This is a higher figure than the 4,122 given in Samuel Lewis's *Topographical Dictionary* (1831).

[15] Additional donations included a contribution from the well-known cleric Sydney Smith. Lambeth Palace Library, ICBS 1401 St Mary Hornsey, 21ff.

[16] I. Roscoe, *A Biographical Dictionary of Sculptors in Britain, 1660-1851*, Yale University Press, 2009, p. 995.

[17] The Act to amend burial of the dead beyond the limits of the metropolis was discussed by the Hornsey Vestry on 7 Sept. 1854. It also required that only one body be buried in each grave, except in family vaults. Vestry Minutes from Nov. 1834, Bruce Castle Museum.

[18] LMA DRO 20/B2/18.

[19] The 'common mortar' specified was 'strong well-burnt stone lime from Merstham, Dorking or Guildford, mixed with clear sharp drift river sand in proportions of 3:1 (sand to lime); Roman cement mortar: half cement; half sand.'

[20] Bruce Castle, St Mary Hornsey Vestry minutes 1834-1860.

[21] Examples of tall belfries of this time, among many, are the London churches of Lewis Vulliamy: Christ Church Woburn Square, St Michael Highgate, St Bartholomew Sydenham. Was there some conscious rivalry with Highgate?

6.1 St Mary Hornsey and its churchyard, drawing in Robinson, *History of Hornsey*. Manuscript (Bruce Castle Museum)

CHAPTER 6

The Nineteenth Century: Canon Harvey's Church

In 1833 the contrast between the homely but crowded atmosphere of the old church and the lofty spaciousness of the new must have seemed extreme. The difference in height can still be seen from the old and new gable lines visible on the east wall of the tower [fig. 6.2]. But to appreciate the new interior we have to rely on comparisons and illustrations. The most striking comparison available is George Smith's other church, St Michael Blackheath, which is happily little altered from its early nineteenth century state [fig. 6.3]. St Michael's fanciful east tower is another matter, but its tall, light, interior with galleried aisles behind slim Gothic arches appears remarkably similar to the impression given by surviving views of St Mary Hornsey [fig.

6.2 Tower east wall, with the gable lines of the medieval church and its 1833 replacement

75

6.4]. These churches were essentially 'preaching boxes' in an elegant Gothic dress. Both churches were designed with similarly arranged sanctuaries, with a fashionable pinnacled Gothic structure behind the altar forming a frame for the traditional sacred texts.

Interior views of St Mary's show plain rendered walls with incised lines imitating stonework. The roof was concealed by a flat plaster ceiling, with bosses at the intersections of the moulded ribs, as prescribed in the specification. A watercolour view looking west shows all the ceiling beams painted brown [fig. 6.5], but the small amateur painting looking east shows the ceiling with the mouldings and bosses white against a dark ground. The character of this ceiling can be gauged from the surviving ceiling in the tower, which retains its ribs and foliage bosses of plaster (as well as the circular opening for the bells referred to in the accounts).[1] The bosses, decorated with varieties of stylised foliage, are an interesting early effort at medieval detail, but moulded in plaster, not carved in stone or wood as was the practice of later Gothic Revival craftsmen [fig. 6.6]. The views also show that there was further decorative detail on capitals of the main shafts of the columns and along the string course above, probably also in plaster.

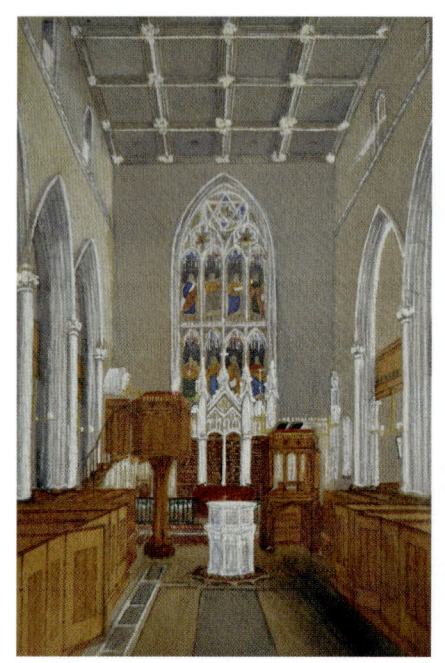

6.3 St Michael Blackheath, architect George Smith, interior looking east

6.4 St Mary Hornsey in the mid nineteenth century, interior looking east, painting (St Mary with St George)

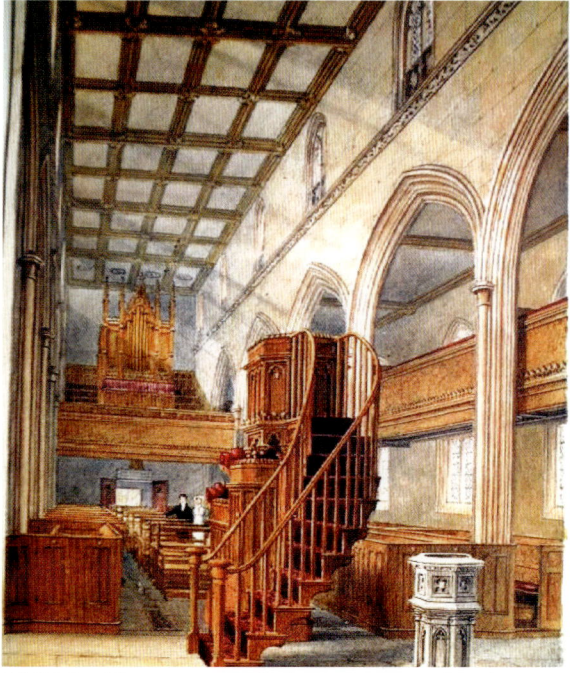

6.5 St Mary Hornsey, interior looking west, watercolour (present location unknown)

Both the paintings indicate that the old font was placed centrally, toward the east end, but differ over the position of the pulpit. There was considerable debate at this period about the ideal pulpit position. The view looking west shows an elaborate three-decker construction (pulpit, reading desk and clerk's desk) placed centrally, as on the plan submitted to the Incorporated Church Building Society; reminiscences of around 1850 confirm this arrangement, describing how the rector at the afternoon service catechised the children 'sitting around the three-decker which then occupied a position in the centre of the church in front of the Communion rails'.[2] The obscuring of the altar by the pulpit was objected to by those who considered that it appeared to privilege preaching over prayer, and by the later nineteenth century the pulpit stood to one side, as in the painting looking east and in later photographs. The principal seating was provided by traditional box pews; rather awkward temporary benches in the broad central aisle can be seen in in the view looking west.

6.6 Plaster bosses of 1833 in the tower

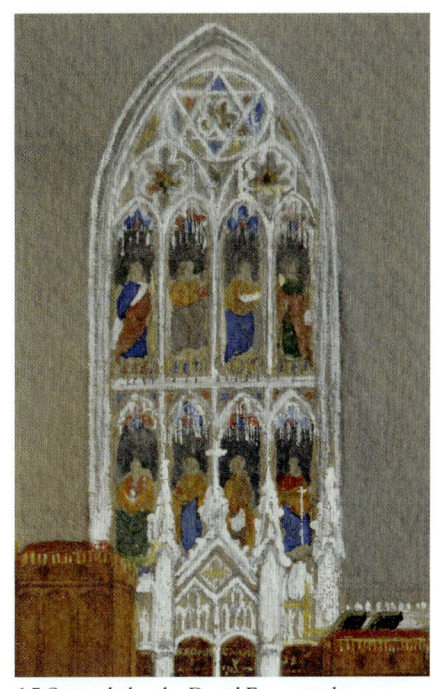

A further embellishment deserves notice. The painting looking east shows a brightly coloured east window [fig 6.7]. A note in the *Gentleman's Magazine* of 1835 describes it as newly installed, a work by the stained glass artist David Evans of Shrewsbury, with eight full-length figures of evangelists and saints on Gothic pedestals. The

6.7 Stained glass by David Evans in the east window, of c. 1833 (detail from fig. 6.3)

article comments enthusiastically: 'the mystery of this beautiful art, once considered entirely lost, has been effectively revived by Mr Evans'.[3] David Evans (1793–1861) became known in the 1820s/30s for his work on the restoration of old windows and is now recognised as one of the pioneers in rediscovering stained glass techniques.[4] The introduction of religious figure subjects in an east window, emphasising the significance of the east end of the building, anticipated the popularity of such embellishment in the next decades. The small painting, though sketchy, effectively conveys the vivid colours characteristic of Evans' work (soon to be condemned as crude as skills in stained glass-making developed further). Other glass existed as well in 1835, for the article also mentions side windows with the arms of the Bishop of London and of C. W. Towers Esq. Later references mention

6.8 Interior of the 1833 church, looking east (Potter Collection, British Museum)

other heraldic glass.[5] Heraldic art was a traditional way of acknowledging donors, but it is unknown who commissioned the east window and selected the artist.

In 1850 the Vestry minutes record that the rector requested certain alterations to improve sittings for the poor and the arrangement of the Communion table, but details are not given.[6] Photos of the interior show a decorative lettered board, 'Fight the Good Fight', placed across the reredos but otherwise there seem to have been no major changes to the area around the altar [fig. 6.8]. Apart from the introduction of gas lighting in 1852, funded by public subscription, and the moving of the pulpit, the church remained little changed from the 1830s, and seems to have satisfied Richard Harvey, who trod a tactful middle route between Evangelism on the one hand and High Church ritual on the other, remaining popular and respected throughout the fifty years he was rector. His outstanding qualities were acknowledged in a magnificent testimonial volume presented to him in 1879, which refers not only to his church building but to recognition of his merits beyond Hornsey and by those outside the Church of England.[7]

It appears that all the early monuments recorded in the eighteenth century were transferred from the old building, as promised in the building specification, showing that conscientious attention had been given to the antiquarian concerns expressed before the rebuilding. The Musters monument retained a position on the north wall close to the altar [see fig. 3.14]. The memorials to past rectors were joined by a column commemorating Lewis Atterbury, moved from Highgate Chapel (see Chapter 4).[8] Close by, to the south of the altar, was a wall plaque with portrait relief by the sculptor W. Behnes, erected to the poet Samuel Rogers, who died in 1855 and was buried in a family grave in the extreme north-east corner of the churchyard [fig. 6.9]. Older wall tablets to those of lesser note were crowded on to the west wall under the gallery at the back of the nave. The tradition of wall memorials continued; they included one to the parents of Henry Warner, Jacob and Eliza Warner of The Priory, who died in 1831 and 1833 [fig. 6.10]. The inscription, in a simple Gothic frame matching the style of the new church, records that they were 'pious, just and benevolent, they lived in honour and died in peace'.

THE ARTISTIC RESPONSES

The early views of the church designed by George Smith indicate how different artists responded to this change to a familiar landscape. Henry Bachelor, aged ten when the church was rebuilt, recalled that he was deeply upset by the demolition, and made many efforts to draw it from memory.[9] But the rebuilt church continued to be a popular subject for artists. An early effort to depict the new church is a pencil sketch within Robinson's unpublished *History of Hornsey*, entitled 'Hornsey New Church' [fig. 6.1, chapter heading, page 75].[10] The lightly sketched trees and the hill rising behind the church, seen from the south-east, suggest the rural surroundings, and the ancient character of the churchyard is indicated by a scatter of old tombstones. The church has the look of a building not yet quite at home in its setting. Its height dominates the old churchyard; the ventilator grilles to the crypt appear close to ground level, the tall aisle windows some way above light both the aisle and the gallery. The shallow chancel is flanked by two slim corner buttresses rising as small turrets on either side of the eastern gable. The size of the building is dramatised by the unconvincingly diminutive figure of the grave digger below the east window.

6.9 Wall monument to Samuel Rogers (died 1855), by W. Behnes (Potter Collection British Museum)

6.10 Warner memorial (photograph, private collection)

An undated lithograph, 'on stone by L. Haghe from a drawing by B. Ferrey architect in the possession of the Revd. R. Harvey, rector' [fig. 6.11] shows a more distant view of St Mary's, seen from across the High Road, effectively demonstrating the balance between the body of the church and the heightened tower with its taller north-west turret, which had so pleased the Vestry committee. The darker stone of the tower is faintly indicated, in contrast to the brick walls of the rest of the building. An elaborately flowery inscription explains that the view is ' by permission inscribed to the Right Honble. and Right Rev. Charles James Blomfield DD Lord Bishop of London by his humble servant Benjamin Ferrey'. Ferrey was born in 1810; from 1826 he was a pupil of the architectural draughtsman Auguste Pugin, and later the biographer of Auguste and his more famous son, A. W. N. Pugin, Ferrey's contemporary. The view of St Mary's may have been made in the 1830s, early in Ferrey's career as an architect, the dedication perhaps suggesting a hope that the bishop might assist him in gaining commissions for other new churches.[11] The informal hedge and rustic gate indicate the drawing was made during or immediately after the rebuilding, before the installation of the new churchyard gate and entrance mentioned in the final accounts presented in 1835. The details in the foreground are in the tradition of older picturesque views, but this is a forthright declaration of how a modern church should look, a model for the future, exemplified by the building erected on the Bishop of London's former manor. The rector's living conditions were also the subject of improvement. Ferrey's sketch of the rectory rebuilt for Richard Harvey shows a villa whose Tudor style suggests strongly that this too was designed by George Smith [fig. 6.12]. It lay west of the church on the north side of the High Street, recalled now by the road named Rectory Gardens, which ran around its grounds. The building in the distance of fig. 6.11 may represent the rectory, viewed (with some geographical licence) across the glebe land.

6.11 St Mary Hornsey from the north-east, lithograph by Benjamin Ferrey (British Museum)

6. CANON HARVEY'S CHURCH

6.16 Hornsey Church from the north-west, lithograph by Thomas Packer, 1859 (British Museum)

The concept of the romance of towers hidden in greenery has a long literary history, from 'towers and battlements … bosomed high in tufted trees' in Milton's *L'Allegro* to 'yonder ivy-mantled tow'r' in Thomas Gray's *Elegy Written in a Country Churchyard*. The softening effect of greenery on and around the tower was an effective disguise and views show that by the later nineteenth century the ivy extended to the rest of the building as well. Was it deliberately encouraged? There was a growing enthusiasm for ivy among the Victorians, heightened by a book on the subject by the popular garden writer Shirley Hibberd, published in 1872.[17]

In an early photograph of 1870 the church stands on its own with open land to the west, the tower entirely covered in ivy, which has been cut back to allow only a view of the clock, west window and belfry window [fig. 6.17]. That impression was endorsed in Thorne's *Handbook to the Environs of London*, published the same year with a somewhat dismissive description: 'The church looks better at a distance than close at hand. The old ivy-covered tower is an attractive object from the neighbouring heights and picturesque when near, but the

6.17 Hornsey Church, 1870 (Potter Collection, British Museum)

83

6.18 Hornsey tower in greenery, etching 1879 by Edwin Roffe after a drawing of 1859 (British Museum)

body of the church is brick and Gothic of the year 1833.' However, the author adds: 'the interior of the church is kept in excellent order'.[18] The enfolding greenery can be seen also in an etching signed by printmaker and engraver Edwin Roffe where only the top of the tower can be seen above the cluster of holly trees to its north-west (the trees still remain) [fig. 6.18].

THE CHURCHYARD

A vignette of Hornsey Churchyard in *The Illustrated News of the World* shows a neat array of family chest tombs, perhaps intended as a sober *memento mori* for the respectable family perambulating the churchyard [fig. 6.19].[19] The image of Hornsey churchyard as an ancient and atmospheric place of burial was sufficiently well known to have a fictional mention in Charles Dickens's *David Copperfield*.[20] The family tomb of the then very popular poet Samuel Rogers, who died in 1855, author (among other works) of *The Pleasures of Memory*, gave Hornsey an added literary cachet [fig. 8.19]. Thorne's *Environs of London* noted the tradition of the churchyard's 'secluded and rural air' and that it had always been 'a favourite with those who love to meditate among the tombs, (an allusion to James Hervey's well-known 'Meditations among the Tombs' of 1745).[21]

There was some effort to regulate burials. Soon after the rebuilding, the Vestry agreed that there was to be no new grave within 20 feet of the church walls, and none were to be less than 6 feet deep. A table of fees was agreed, with fees to be double for non-parishioners.[22] But as demand for burial space increased, the lack of space in the churchyard became acute, as is shown in a detailed survey made in 1839 [fig. 6.20]. The plan by the surveyor J. H. Taylor shows how the two east-west lines of large chest tombs above vaults had smaller graves packed tightly around them, while others filled the space up to the boundaries. The problem was tackled by extending the churchyard to the south, using the land beyond the boundary path shown on the right side of the plan, and creating the churchyard which survives today. The extension came into use in 1839 and the first graves were laid out in a neat north-to-south row along its eastern border, starting with a traditional family tomb chest to the Taylor family, and continuing with a series of large, boldly lettered ledger

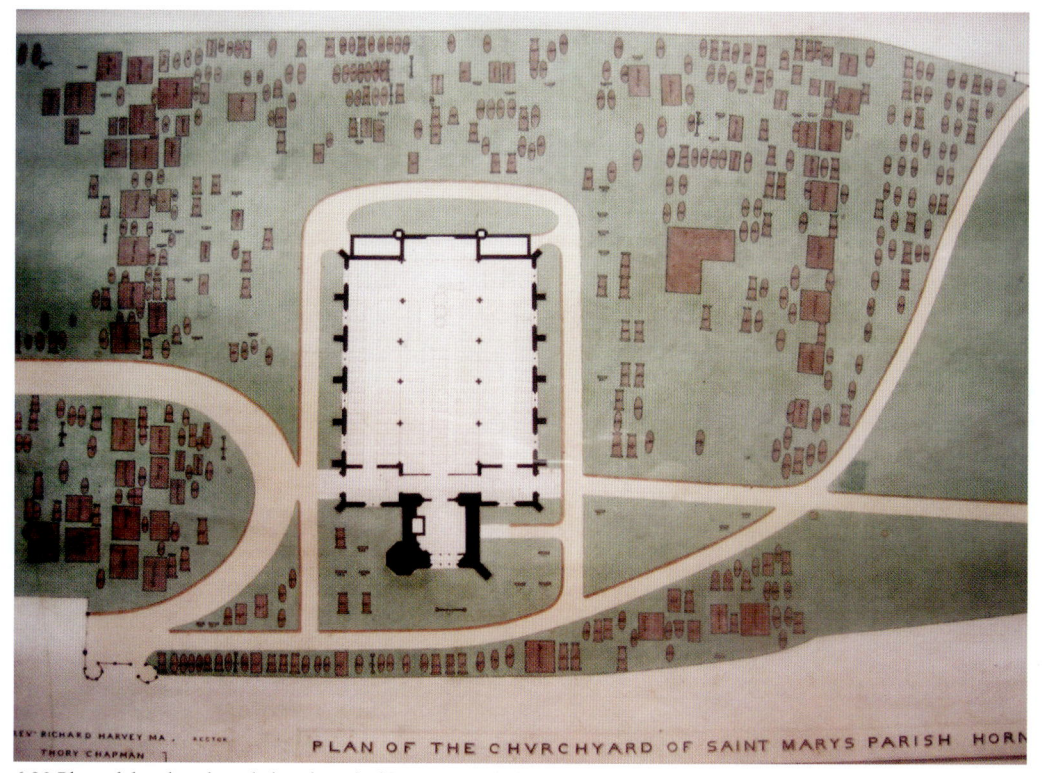

6.19 Hornsey Church from the south-east, *Illustrated News of the World*, 1858 (British Museum)

6.20 Plan of the church and churchyard of St Mary's Parish, Hornsey 1839 by J. H. Taylor (LMA DRO/020/B/03/002)

stones [fig. 6.21]. The most remarkable of these is the tomb of Harriet Long and Jacob Walker. As the inscription explains, Jacob Walker was 'in America the faithful slave, in England the faithful servant' of Harriet Long. They both died in 1840; the monument was provided by Harriet's husband, George Long, Professor of Greek History at the University of London, and includes a Latin poem extolling his wife's virtues [fig. 6.22].[23] This row of tombs now lies partly hidden among the trees and undergrowth around the edge of the churchyard. To the west the ground has been cleared and the churchyard extension has only a few reminders of the more varied types of memorial favoured by the Victorians during the five decades when it was in use as a burial ground.[24]

6.21 The first tombs in the churchyard extension in use from 1839

Later monuments took diverse forms, sometimes including standing crosses (previously considered too Popish), or inscription plaques raised on pedestals and surrounded by kerbstones. Such monuments were vulnerable to later vandalism and few survive. Old photos give a general impression showing how crowded the churchyard had become by the end of the century [fig. 6.23].[25] Burials after 1840 were not confined to the extension; many were fitted in among the older memorials. To the east of the church squeezed in beside older monuments, a new tomb chest was erected for William Pattinson 'of Stroud Green' (died 1844) [fig. 6.24]. The lettering is in Gothic script, but the top of the chest was originally adorned with a classical urn, discovered in 2009.[26] This was uncommon, since in general monuments at Hornsey were less ornate than those in private burial grounds such as Highgate Cemetery, which from the 1830s offered an alternative place of rest for more affluent local residents.

6.22 Tomb of Harriet Long and Jacob Walker, 1840

6.23 Church and churchyard from the south, late nineteenth century (Hornsey Historical Society)

As new memorials increased, many of the older standing tombstones, increasingly illegible, disappeared. An unusual entry in the Vestry minutes of 1854 records respect for an older monument: a decision to repair the tomb of Daniel Midwinter 'now in a ruinous condition … as the said Daniel Midwinter was a generous benefactor to this parish'. The cost was to be met by asking the Stationers' Company to divert one of their usual £7 payments for apprenticeship fees for this purpose.[27]

Nineteenth century tombstones often bore quite elaborate and individual inscriptions, giving more than just names and dates. Relatively few inscriptions are now completely legible, but fortunately their variety can be studied in records made by F. T. Cansick c. 1870[28] and by the North Middlesex Family History Society in 1989 (see further Chapter 8), which have preserved details of many now lost. As with earlier tombs, people were often defined not only by a place of residence in or near Hornsey or Highgate, but also by their place of origin. Pattinson's inscription records that he was born at Penrith, Cumberland. The ledger of the geologist and local government campaigner Joshua Toulmin Smith 'of Birmingham and of Highgate', who died in 1869, reflects its subject's diligent activity with its unusual quotation

6.24 Chest tomb of William Pattinson, died 1844

87

from the Epistle of St James – 'he being not a forgetful hearer but a doer of the work'. Although 'of this parish' appears on many tombs, the churchyard appealed to a wider catchment. Some tombs mention neighbouring areas such as Tottenham and Stoke Newington, or central London addresses, indications of a fluid society where professional people had more than one base, or who retired to Hornsey after working in town. Inscriptions mention origins in many other English counties as well as Wales, Scotland and Ireland, a reminder that while the metropolis was attracting people from all over the British Isles, their place of origin remained important to them. There is scope for much more research in relating addresses and places of burial in this period.

6.25 Granite tombs; William and Elizabeth Block (died 1861 and 1880); Mark Beauchamp Peacock (died 1861)

The extension provided space for the most aspiring monuments commemorating those who had recently established themselves as local gentry. The most prominent examples in the western border include several of polished Scottish granite, available after the development of rail transport, a hard-wearing material which had the advantage of withstanding polluted atmosphere. A massive tomb to Mark Beauchamp Peacock (died 1861), Solicitor to the Post Office, stands next to a lower tomb to William and Elizabeth Block (died 1861 and 1880) [fig. 6.25].[29] Nearby is a coped Gothic tombstone to the Revd. William Snell (died 1854) [fig. 6.26]. Elaborately Gothic memorials remained the exception, although tombstones with curved Gothic heads became frequent. Others were even simpler; the plainest of slabs commemorates the Dutch poet and schoolmaster of Cromwell House, Highgate, Gerard van de Linde Monteuuis (1808–1858).[30]

From 1872 new graves were forbidden and, from 1892, no burials were allowed. Among those in the last period was that of William Poulton, who died in 1888 aged 80 and was buried with his wife who had died in 1859. The substantial red granite tombstone,

6.26 Coped tomb of Revd. William Snell, died 1854

whose inscription refers to the 'much respected inhabitant of this parish' [fig. 6.27] stands close to the north-west entrance to the churchyard, not too far from the celebrated Three Compasses where Poulton had been innkeeper. An evocative winter photograph of 1889 by W. H. Thompson shows the still undeveloped area of the High Street between the church and the Three Compasses [fig. 6.28]. A few years later the once rural inn was rebuilt and a terrace with shops lined the south side of the High Street all the way to the churchyard. The distant trees in Thompson's photograph conceal another radical change. Beyond them lay the great roof of a new church. A new chapter in the history of St Mary's had begun.

6.27 Tomb of William Poulton, died 1888

6.28 Hornsey High Street, photograph by W. H. Thompson, 1889 (NMPS Collection, Hornsey Historical Society)

1. Investigation of paint fragments from the tower ceiling indicates that the original paint was a stone colour (Ian Bristow, personal communication).

2. 'Hornsey Village around 1850', reprinted from *Hornsey Journal*, 1905, *Hornsey Historical Society Bulletin* 21, 1980, pp. 7–11.

3. *The Gentleman's Magazine*, October 1835, p. 413.

4. Martin Harrison, *Victorian Stained Glass*, Barrie and Jenkins, 1980, pp. 16–17.

5. [Anon], *The Story of Hornsey Parish Church*, British Publishing Company, Gloucester, 1949, mentions coats of arms, of unknown date, to the Booths of Crouch Hall, Edward Chapman of Harringay House, Charles Scrase Dickens of Grove Lodge, Muswell Hill, Lord Mansfield of Kenwood and William Howley, Archbishop of Canterbury 1818–48, previously Bishop of London. There were also some fragments of old glass gathered together in a window above the south door (B. M. Potter coll. note 1887).

6. St Mary Hornsey, Vestry minutes begun November 1834, Bruce Castle Museum

7. Obituary of Harvey in *Gloucester Chronicle*, 1889 (Potter Collection, BM Prints and Drawings). See also the favourable comments by Henry Bachelor in *Gin and Hellfire: Henry Batchelor's Memoirs of a Working Class Childhood in Crouch End 1823–1837*, ed. Peter Barber, Hornsey Historical Society, 2004, p. 44. The testimonial is illustrated in Ken Gay, *Hornsey and Crouch End*, The Archive Photographs series, Chalford Publishing Co. 1998, p.15 (reprinted by The History Press, 2008). The new churches during Harvey's time were: St James Muswell Hill (1840–46), Christ Church Crouch End (1861–62 with several later extensions), All Saints Highgate (1864), Holy Innocents, close to St Mary's in Tottenham Lane (1877). In the 1880s, others followed: Holy Trinity Stroud Green (1880) and a temporary iron church of 1884, St Peter Wightman Road, for the fast growing streets of the 'Harringay ladder' west of Green Lanes.

8. The monuments which were in the church c. 1870 are listed by F. T. Cansick, *A Collection of Curious and Interesting Epitaphs Copied from the Existing Monuments of Distinguished and Noted Characters in the Churches and Churchyards of Hornsey…*, London, 1875.

9. Barber, *Gin and Hellfire*, p. 38 (p. 74 n.4).

10. William Robinson, *Collections for a History and Antiquities of the Parish of Hornsey…* MSS, Bruce Castle Museum 17854Ph.

11. On Ferrey see B. F. L. Clarke, *Church Builders of the Nineteenth Century*, London, 1938. From the 1840s onwards Ferrey had a wide practice but built relatively few churches in London. His best known was St Stephen Rochester Row, Westminster, of 1847.

12. Bernard Adams, *London Illustrated 1604–1851*, Oryx Press, 1983, lists ten examples of guide books with illustrations of Hornsey Church, half of them dating from after the rebuilding.

13. *VCH Middlesex*, vol. VI, pp. 168–72.

14. John H. Brady, *A New Pocket Guide to London and its Environs*, John W. Parker, London, 1838, p.359.

15. Note on Thomas Packer, Prints and Drawings Department, British Museum Collections Online, visited 30 January 2015.

16. One of the substantial timber gateposts is now in the tower basement.

17. See Peter Q. Rose, *The Gardener's Guide to Growing Ivies*, Timber Press, 1996, pp.14–21.

18. James Thorne, *Handbook to the Environs of London*, John Murray, London, 1876, pp. 363–4.

19. *Illustrated News of the World*, 3 July 1858.

20. Published 1850. Dickens names Hornsey as the burial place of the husband of David Copperfield's great-aunt Betsy Trotwood.

21. Thorne, *Handbook*, p. 364.

22. Vestry minutes, 19 November 1834, Bruce Castle archives

23. R. Hidson, 'The Lady and the Slave, a Hornsey Mystery', *Hornsey Historical Society Bulletin* 27, 1986, pp. 10–12. In recognition of its connection with the history of emancipation, the tomb was Listed Grade II in 2008.

24. Eric Robinson, *Geology from a Churchyard: A Tombstone Trail Round St Mary's, Hornsey*, Hornsey Historical Society, 2000.

25. Nineteenth-century views appear to give somewhat contradictory impressions of the churchyard tombs, partly no doubt due to artistic licence and to foreshortening of views from the south.

26. The urn, in two halves, was discovered beside the tomb during the tomb survey carried out in 2009–11.

27. A tomb 'in memory of Daniel Midwinter' with the date 1857 was recorded by the North Middlesex Family History Society in 1987 in the western border.

28. Cansick, *A Collection of Curious and Entertaining Epitaphs*.

29. The Peacock home was Southwood, a villa in Southwood Lane, Highgate, famous for its fine grounds.

30. For more details on individual tombs see Joan Schwitzer, *Buried in Hornsey: The Graves of St Mary's Churchyard*, and Eric Robinson, *Geology from a Churchyard*, both published by Hornsey Historical Society, 2000. On van de Linde see Marita Mathijsen, 'Gerrit van de Linde: A Dutch Poet and Schoolmaster in Highgate', *Hornsey Historical Society Bulletin* 47, 2006, pp. 2–7.

7.1 Hornsey, Ordnance Survey map 1891, showing the old church and its new, incomplete, successor

CHAPTER 7

A Century of Change

JAMES JEAKES' CHURCH

By 1890 George Smith's church was no longer in use and a replacement had been erected on the glebe land to the east. Richard Harvey, from 1858 a canon of Gloucester Cathedral, had retired aged 80 in 1879 and moved to Gloucester. His successor, the Revd. James Jeakes, was of a different mould and eager for change. He had previously been Vicar of St Matthias Bethnal Green, in one of the poorest areas of London, and so was familiar with the challenges of contemporary urban society. Hornsey was now a commuter suburb on the edge of London, well connected by public transport, a very different place from the village of fifty years before. By 1881 the population was 37,000 compared with 3,925 in 1851.[1] The older established families were disappearing; mansions and villas gave way to terrace houses for the less affluent [fig. 7.1]. The 1880s–90s saw the development of both the Warner estate centred on The Priory and its grounds, and the Harringay House estate west of Green Lanes.[2] In Harvey's time, new churches had already been built elsewhere in the parish for the new middle-class residents and all these competed with a growing number of nonconformist places of worship.

Apart from the need to cater for demographic change, anyone concerned at this time with Anglican church building would have considered George Smith's church as very old-

91

7.2 Appeal leaflet for the new church 1887 (Potter Collection, British Museum)

fashioned. A more sophisticated understanding of Gothic had been encouraged by the writings of Pugin and his followers; from the 1840s, Gothic of the thirteenth and fourteenth centuries was the preferred inspiration for new churches. Under the joint influence of the Oxford Movement and the Cambridge ecclesiologists there was increasing emphasis on creating a more ample setting for altar and choir at the east end, for abolishing galleries, and housing all the congregation on the ground floor with easy access to the east end for the now more frequent Communion services. Many older churches were enlarged for this purpose; the medieval All Hallows in neighbouring Tottenham, for example, was radically remodelled by William Butterfield in 1875–77 by the addition of new transepts and a large chancel.

St Mary's was clearly seen to be deficient in having no chancel, only a very modest sanctuary. A solution might have been simply to extend the building to the east. But in 1887 Jeakes wrote to the ICBS to ask for help in building a completely new church: 'Hornsey is not what it was and is becoming poorer every year. Our offertories get smaller continually and there are very few rich people left. It is a great work greatly needed but unless we get large help from the outside I don't see how it is to be done … We do not intend to pull down the old church although of course we intend to shut it up. One day it may be wanted as well as the new…' He added that the existing church had seats divided between around 100 families, with free seats at the backs of the galleries, whereas there were now 1,600 families in the district; 'the working classes are therefore practically shut out from the Church'.[3]

Rebuilding on a new site avoided the need to disturb existing graves, and involved minimum disruption to church services. The appeal leaflet explained that the adjoining glebe land to the east was being made available for a church to seat 1,200, with at least half the seats free, and that 'the present church with its ancient tower can remain as a memorial of the past, and the bells, for the present at least, will be left in the old tower'. The impressive view of the proposed building by the architect James Brooks (1825–1901) included a magnificent tower and spire, which it was hoped to complete later [fig. 7.2].

The architect and style selected departed from the tradition established in Hornsey in the 1860s, when the architect A. W. Blomfield (son of the bishop, the rector's friend) had adopted a sober version of thirteenth century Gothic for the new churches of Christ Church Crouch End and All Saints Highgate, and, later, for Holy Innocents Tottenham Lane. James Brooks was well known for his impressively lofty East End churches of the late 1860s and more recently for his south London landmark, the Church of the Ascension on Lavender Hill, Battersea (which, like Hornsey, was intended to have a commanding tower which was never built). Brooks followed the new trend, which developed from around 1870, for vast urban churches intended to cater for all levels of society, not just the comfortable middle classes.[4] The style which he chose for Hornsey was 'Perpendicular' Gothic, exemplified by the great late medieval churches of East Anglia, a safely traditional choice, in contrast to his more adventurous use of continental late Gothic for the exactly contemporary All Hallows Gospel Oak. Although Perpendicular had become popular with other architects at this time, it was Brooks' only use of the style; was it chosen in deference to the light, airy spaces of George Smith's church and perhaps even to reminiscences of its predecessor? Above the altar was a wide seven-light window, high up, to allow space for a reredos below. Inside, the tall, handsomely moulded arcade arches were generously broad, allowing maximum visibility from the aisles; there was no division, apart from steps, between chancel and nave. The superior quality of St Mary's was to be marked by facing the building in stone rather than the cheaper brick used for Brooks' churches in the East End.

Because of the shape of the site the church was designed untraditionally, on a north-south axis, with the proposed tower over the entrance from the High Street. The bold effort to find the money was initially successful [fig. 7.3]; by 1888 £7,700 had been raised – although more was needed – and the foundations were dug.[5] By 30 June the *Hornsey Journal* reported that 'the masons are hewing the pretty Ancaster stones which are to form the external walls … and bricklayers are busy rearing the underground walls'. When the church was consecrated in November 1889 by the Bishop of London, Frederick Temple, the entrance front was still incomplete. The debts incurred by the building costs were repaid by 1895, leaving £200-£300 to start a fund for completing the work.[6]

7.3 Collection box in aid of the new building

7.4 The new church by James Brooks from the south-east; the old tower visible beyond on the left (Historic England)

As promised, half of the 1,200 seats were free; in contrast to those in the earlier church these free seats were described as 'equally good' as the other half, which were also free, but 'appropriated'. The rector hoped that all services would be 'reverend, bright and hearty' and requested that as the seats were free, there would be increased contributions to the offertory.[7]

BELL-RINGING

At the turn of the century the old church was a disused relic smothered in ivy, the centrepiece of the crowded but now no longer used churchyard. It was much reproduced on contemporary postcards, cherished as a relic of 'old Hornsey'. The bells in the tower continued in use. From 1833 the bell-ringers had the benefit of their own access to the refurbished ringing chamber through the door in the basement, and the existence of a flourishing ringing community is demonstrated by the record of a 'ringers' jug', inscribed with the popular couplet from the third bell (see Chapter 4) and the words 'presented by James Brett, Ringer, to the Society of Hornsey Ringers'.[8] Surviving ringers' boards testify to continuing activity. In 1880 one of Jeakes' first acts as rector had been to improve the bells dating from the 1770s. The tenor bell had been recast, as was recorded on an inscription on the bell: 'this bell was recast and the other five bells tuned by John Warner and Sons. James Jeakes M. A. Rector, Gilbert Robins, John Martin, churchwardens'. A ringing board still in the tower records the peals rung on Sunday evening 9 October 1881: Plain Bob Minor and Grandsire Minor 'supposed to be the first rung upon these bells' [fig. 7.5a]. The ringers were the prestigious Royal Cumberland Youths; beneath their names are those of the rector, churchwardens and 'G. Griffin, steeplekeeper'. A Bellringers Guild was formed in 1891 'for cultivating the art of change ringing as an

7. A CENTURY OF CHANGE

exercise among the parishioners'.[9] The two later surviving boards, from 1903 and 1912, respectively recall peals rung by the Middlesex County Association and the Hornsey Guild, the latter consisting of Plain Bob Minor (1912 changes rung in one hour eleven minutes, composed and conducted by C. H. Ross) [figs. 7.5b, 7.5c].

After the building of the new church the congregation no longer passed through the churchyard, as the main approaches were from the High Street or Church Lane. Up to 1891 the churchyard was kept in good order through the efforts of Gilbert Robins (rector's churchwarden for seventeen years). After he moved away from Hornsey there was a rapid decline; in 1893 there were complaints about cracked paths, hedges, fences and gates in a disgraceful state and about a dust-heap beside the tomb of Samuel Rogers. For the next few years the churchwardens employed the appropriately named firm of William Cutbush & Son of Highgate Nurseries to cut the grass, care for the paths and pick up paper on Sunday mornings before 10 a.m.[10] His successor was a (less expensive) Mr McGregor, but this arrangement ended in 1897. Previously upkeep had been paid out of a charitable fund administered by the Overseers for the Poor which had been set up with money from the sale of 'Church Field' to the Great Northern Railway, but the Overseers were reluctant to pay for the expensive walls or railings now considered necessary as the surrounding land became built up. The Hornsey District Council, enlightened and responsible in its care for other public amenities, stepped in. In 1895 it agreed to take on the repair of the churchyard with maintenance carried out by the Council's workforce.[11] A decision to erect railings was reported in the *Hornsey Journal* on 11 December 1897: 'the pattern of the fence to be approved of by the rector, the price not exceeding 5s per foot run'. A Borough of Hornsey noticeboard was erected beside spear-headed railings along the paths entered from the High Street, Temple Road and Church Lane. The paths were no longer reminiscent of the rural past; they had become part of the new urban fabric, treated as public rights of way and lit by street lamps. Fragments of the railings still survive on the eastern side of the main path running south from the High Street [fig 7.6].

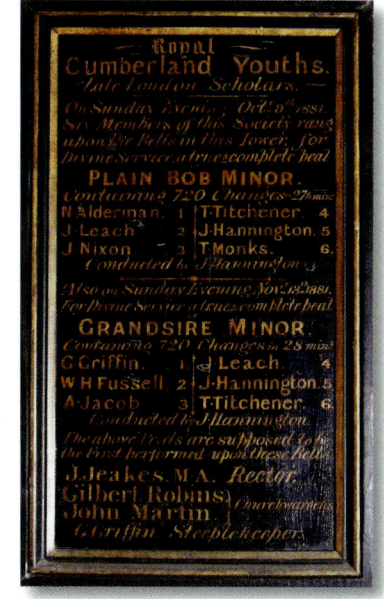

7.5a Ringers' board in the bell-ringing chamber, 1881

7.5b Ringers' board in the bell-ringing chamber, 1903

7.5c Ringers' board in the bell-ringing chamber, 1912

7.6 Churchyard railings of c. 1900

At the beginning of the twentieth century the Anglican Church remained an enthusiastic patron of the Gothic Revival. The new St Mary's was given its intended grand entrance facing the High Street, through the base of the proposed tower. The extension was dedicated in June 1900 by the Bishop of London, Mandell Creighton. Porches on either side, providing entrances from Church Lane and from the churchyard, were completed in 1911 and 1914 [fig 7.7].[12] For the new work the parish did not return to James Brooks but employed a different architect, Sir Charles Nicholson, although following the plan proposed by Brooks. Nicholson had been a pupil of J. D. Sedding, and from the 1890s with his partner H. C. Corlette built up a reputation as a church architect involved with both new buildings and alterations. His additions gave the church a greater presence on the High Street, but the commanding spire which had been proposed by Brooks remained a dream.

Nicholson's extensions had a smooth elegance quite different from Brooks' rugged masonry. The substantial square base, intended to support a tower, was of plain ashlar blocks, relieved by blind tracery and some sculptural decoration around the central entrance and modest corner pinnacles on the angle buttresses [fig. 7.7]. The lower side-porches had decorative window surrounds and pierced parapets. Nicholson believed that Gothic was unavoidable for contemporary church building, but he was sympathetic to the need to build economically. In a later essay he warned of the dangers of attempting too much: 'If one has to build for a low price, don't think of towers, or even of bell cots.'[13] Did his experience at Hornsey inspire this

7.7 St Mary's seen from the High Street, with the Nicholson extension; the old tower is on the right (Historic England)

comment? It became clear already in 1904 that the unstable ground made a tower inadvisable, even had the funding been available. There was to be no proud landmark for Hornsey, an absence perhaps felt even more keenly when the prominent spire of St James Muswell Hill rose on the horizon in 1909–10.

Only monochrome photographs are available to convey the architectural grandeur of the interior conceived in the 1880s. When first opened there was little apart from the essential furnishings: a sanctuary with altar, a communion rail presented by the Hornsey Temperance Society, an oak lectern and teak choir stalls.[14] The biggest expense had been the organ provided by the leading organ firm, Henry Willis & Sons which filled the first bay of the arcade on the left. Over the next

7.8 Chancel of the Brooks church, with the altarpiece of 1907 (Historic England)

forty years, as was the case in so many late Victorian churches, a succession of gifts added colour and splendour.[15] The east window was filled with stained glass to celebrate Queen Victoria's Diamond Jubilee in 1897. Further ornament was encouraged by F. N. Thicknesse, Rector from 1904–11, described as a 'moderate High Churchman' in contrast to his 'ultra Protestant' predecessor, Prebendary James Jeakes.[16] In 1907-08 funds were raised for the large gilded reredos behind the high altar, with an array of figures below canopies, the chancel being raised to accommodate this [fig. 7.8]. The cost of the seventeen statues was met by individual donations.[17] A cross was placed on the altar, and the Sunday School raised money for carving the apostles' heads on the arcade capitals.

The medieval theme was continued at the opposite end of the church by a new font, which was given prominence by a massive wooden canopy suspended from a pulley, inspired by late medieval examples in East Anglia. (The medieval font from the old church, considered too modest for the new building, was given to the new church of St George Priory Road, in 1907.) The tower arch was filled by a glazed Gothic screen in memory of Bishop Mandell Creighton, who died in 1901, and the tower window was given stained glass by Kempe, in memory of James Jeakes, who retired in 1901 and died in 1915. Among the later furnishings installed was a late seventeenth century gilded credence table from the old church, which for a time was in St Luke Mayfield Road.[18]

A significant later addition, typical of the interlocking concerns of Anglicanism and patriotism, was the fitting up of a First World War Memorial Chapel for the 1/7th Battalion

7.9 War Memorial Chapel, furnished by G. H. Fellowes Prynne, 1922 (Historic England)

of the Middlesex Regiment, which had lost 66 officers and 780 men in the war. The work was completed in 1922, designed by G. H. Fellowes Prynne, a Gothic Revival architect who came to specialise in war memorials [fig. 7.9]. The first bay of the right-hand aisle was divided off by a screen with openwork tracery. On each side of the double door, on the lower part of each section, were two square panels bearing names in three columns. Above the door was the badge of the Middlesex Regiment. The altar was in the style known as 'Old English', with flanking curtains and posts topped by gilded angels. The tripartite reredos combined panels in mosaic and paint, depicting the resurrected Christ, flanked by St George and St Hubert. Additional wooden boards bore the names of 136 parishioners of St Mary Hornsey who fell in the war.[19]

In the 1920s the new St Mary's was well attended. The rector from 1926–33 was Henry Montgomery Campbell, who later became successively Bishop of Willesden, Kensington, Guildford and London. On 29 April 1927 the *Hornsey Journal* reported a congregation of about 1,200 each Sunday, a vindication of the claim in 1880 that a larger church was needed. But there were signs that all was not well. Hilda Sheppard, later secretary to the Parochial Church Council, born in 1920, wrote that as a little girl she remembered cracks appearing and her father saying that the building should be underpinned.[20] However, a report in 1927 stated that there was no cause for alarm. Repairs needed to the organ were of more immediate concern; after five years of fundraising these were completed in 1928, when an electric blower replaced the original hydraulic mechanism.[21] In 1935 the north arcade was scaffolded in order to repair the cracks (requiring twenty-eight pailfuls of grouting, according to churchwarden Sidey). The chancel was also strengthened, with concrete and steel rods placed below the floor, for which a grant of £500 was received from the City Charities Fund.[22]

THE FATE OF THE OLD CHURCH AND ITS MONUMENTS

Apart from the use of the tower for bell-ringing it appeared that there was no future for the rest of the old church. In 1926 its demolition was announced.[23] The *Hornsey Journal* reported that the building had 'become little more than a ruin. Some long time ago many of the roof beams fell in and, exposed to rain and air, the building is being reduced to a state of decay'. There was an official visit by the Archdeacon of Hampstead and a report by F. C. Eeles, secretary to the Council for the Care of Churches, to the Diocesan Advisory Council. Little sympathy was expressed for George Smith's church, which was described as being 'in the clumsy style of that period', so that 'from an architectural point of view the loss will be a comparatively small one'. The report stated that 'at various times the pulpit, altar and font were taken out and are in use elsewhere' and that the stained glass windows had been removed and monuments transferred. But it also noted that there were other interesting monuments and relics still in the building, some from the old Highgate Chapel. A Faculty was granted for removing and disposing of the old church in April 1927 and demolition followed immediately.[24]

An excitement during the demolition was the Rector's discovery in the crypt of the brass inscription to the two sons of William Priestley (see Chapter 2).[25] A contemporary sketch shows the slender columns of the arcades exposed to the sky, but the stepped west gallery still in place, built up against the wall of the tower [fig. 7.10]. Editorial comment in the *Hornsey Journal* made a clear distinction between the worthless old church which was 'in shockingly bad condition' and the old tower: 'for that there is a sentimental feeling which will be its safeguard even in this materialistic age'[26] – an acknowledgement of the tower's traditional role as symbol of the historic village centre. Although a few correspondents expressed regrets about the loss of the building, in general the demolition appears to have excited little interest. The Hornsey population was now very different from that in Canon Harvey's day. The rural villas of the moneyed middle classes had long disappeared, and so had the personal links with the old church and churchyard of Canon Harvey's era. The burial crypt was filled in and the site of the church levelled to a height slightly above the surrounding paths, leaving fragments of the west walls to buttress the surviving tower, now stripped of its romantic ivy.

7.10 Demolition of George Smith's church, 1927, drawing by Edgar Fincham (Hornsey Historical Society)

As it was accepted that no tower could be added to the new church, some attention was given to the old one. The arch which had opened onto the nave was walled up and fitted with a pair of doors from one of the demolished entrance porches, and a flight of steps built to reach the level of the vestry room. The steps were created from apparently reused stones bearing eight names of nineteenth century local people, but their original site and purpose remains a puzzle.[27] The old vestry within the tower continued to be used occasionally for meetings, by the Boy Scouts and others. Its fireplace (possibly created at this level by George Smith, making use of the older flue leading up from the basement), was at some point given a new surround in modern brick. The bells were repaired in 1930, when new gudgeons and ball bearings were fitted by Mears and Stainbank of the Whitechapel Bell Foundry,[28] and in 1934 new steel beams were inserted to support the old bell frame. The following year a flagstaff was installed in time for King George V's Silver Jubilee. The building was later given new electric wiring, recorded on a neatly designed plaque in the ringing chamber, given in memory of Reginald Peter Crump 'in accordance with his wishes' [fig. 7.11]. A further change was the replacement of the old turret clock mechanism, dating from 1829, by an electric motor.

7.11 Electricity memorial plaque, tower ringing chamber

The churchyard appears to have received intermittent attention; in 1912 tombstones were 'renovated and readjusted', but by 1938 clearance of undergrowth was needed. In 1942 iron railings and old lamp standards were removed for the War Salvage Campaign, which Churchwarden Sidey considered 'much improved the appearance of the churchyard'.[29]

7.12 The tower after the 1927 demolition, with monuments attached on the surviving west wall of the church (Historic England)

THE MONUMENTS

In 1927 some of the ledgers from inside the church were placed on the levelled ground to the east of the tower, and survive in the present Garden of Remembrance. They include the fine stone slab to Francis Musters' grandmother, Lady Basset of Tehidy, of 1682, with a coat of arms. Nine monuments which had been on the west wall inside the church were left in situ, including the elaborate one to Hannah Towers, but exposure and vandalism over the next fifty years have left only a few traces of where they were fixed [fig. 7.12].[30] The parish's annual report of 1927 mentioned that 'by the generosity of a few – one might say a very few, some of the interior memorials had been removed to the new church'.[31] The new porches had provided space where some of the monuments could be housed. Memorials to past rectors were placed in the 'south' (i.e. west) porch, while many of the others, including the wall monument to Francis Musters, were crammed into the 'north' (i.e. east porch) [figs. 7.13, 7.14].[32] A few had already been singled out to be placed on the wall of the 'south' (i.e. west) aisle: the 1602 monument to Richard Candish, consisting of an obelisk with pedestal, the portrait medallion to Samuel Rogers (moved in 1906 at the expense of his relatives), and two tablets in Gothic frames to members of local families – the 1830s monument to Jacob and Eliza Warner (see fig. 6.10) and another to the Revd. Edward Linzee and family [fig. 7.15]. Ironically, none of these specially selected monuments survive. Nor do the ledgers to Jane Musters (1691) and to Francis Musters (1680), which were recorded in 1935 as being 'placed east of the modern church'.[33] The huge George Rey slab was placed in the tower. Six examples of armorial glass from the old church were also installed in the new building.[34]

THE POST-WAR WORLD

Hornsey suffered serious damage in World War Two, affecting over 80 per cent of houses in the borough. In 1941 the Victorian church was damaged by incendiary bombs and in 1944 blast from a rocket bomb (a V2) which fell nearby in the neighbourhood of the

7.13 & 7.14 Wall monuments removed to the Nicholson porches (Historic England)

7.15 South aisle of the Brooks church, with wall monuments from the old church (Historic England)

railway station, affected eaves, gutters, glass and tracery on the Hornsey Station side of the building. War damage money was available for repairs; a report mentioned the need to distinguish these works from the settlement which was now causing cracks above the arcade.[35] The church nevertheless continued to be well supported, organising regular choral festivals from 1949, and celebrating the diamond jubilee of the opening of the new St Mary's in 1889 with a modest but well-researched booklet, *The Story of Hornsey Parish Church*.[36] But by the 1960s there was evidence of more widespread settlement and

7.16 Plan for the Garden of Remembrance, published in Cleary, *Beauty and the Borough*, 1949

by 1967 scaffolding to shore up three of the aisle arches had been introduced as a safety precaution. It was suggested that settlement occurred because the building stood on made-up land created from the dumping of earth during the construction of the railway line.

A GARDEN OF REMEMBRANCE

In the late 1940s efforts were in hand to improve the appearance of the borough, led by Councillor Frederick Cleary. 1949 saw the publication of his slim picture book, *Beauty and the Borough*, with sixty 'before and after' photographs, demonstrating the successes of his amenity campaign, ranging from gardens on bomb sites to window boxes, public seats and well-designed borough notice boards.[37] It starts with a page reprinted from *The Times* (5 August 1948) with a photo of Hornsey Church Tower, 'Hornsey's most historic landmark', and an announcement of a plan for a Garden of Remembrance on the site of the old church. A small sketch (by the Borough Surveyor, J. H. Melville Richards) envisaged an open site with trees, flower beds and a central circular feature, with seats beside the surrounding paths [fig. 7.16]. The book also reproduced John C. Moody's pictorial 'Historic Map of Hornsey' published in 1942, which included a thumbnail sketch of George Smith's church, keeping alive the memory of 'Hornsey old church' and its rural setting [fig. 7.17].

The plan for the churchyard was the most ambitious of Cleary's schemes in Hornsey. A sum of £600 for the garden was raised by the Hornsey War Memorial Committee, under Alderman Mrs C. M. Cave, Hornsey's first woman mayor, in 1947–49. An application for a faculty for the alterations was advertised in 1948.[38] The idea may have been inspired by the campaign to create war memorial gardens on sites of City churches destroyed in the war, proposed in a letter to *The Times* in 1944 and developed further in an attractively illustrated book published by the Architectural Press.[39] The plan adopted at Hornsey, drawn up by J. H. Melville Richards, was rather more mundane: its neat municipal arrangement of bedding plants and dwarf walls made of recycled paving stones was characteristic of many of the small gardens created as part

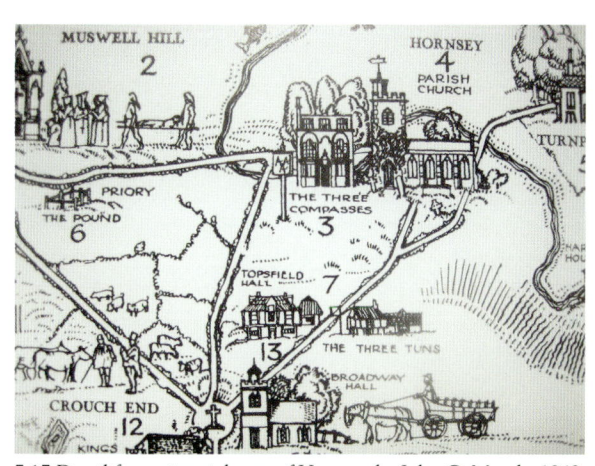

7.17 Detail from pictorial map of Hornsey by John C. Moody, 1942

7.18 Hornsey Churchyard, Remembrance Day 2003, continuing the tradition started in 1950

of Cleary's efforts in Hornsey. But it was undoubtedly a great improvement on the barren railed-off area of the church site. A low wall was erected to the east of the garden to divide it from the rest of the churchyard, incorporating seats facing the tower. The layout with its central path provided an appropriately formal framework for the Remembrance Day celebrations, when wreaths were laid at the top of the steps to the tower. The opening took place on Remembrance Sunday 1950, attended by the 1/7th Battalion of the Middlesex Regiment and their Old Comrades Association. They assembled on the south side. The public gathered on the east and north sides; the Bishop, Rector and choir approached from the new church by a path from the north-east. The ceremony, with gradually dwindling support, continued as an annual event until 2009 [fig. 7.18].[40]

7.19 Plaque erected 1950

The garden was not the only change. The curved holly-lined path from the north-west gate was abandoned and a formal central approach from the High Street was created, with metal gates between stone piers. A bronze circular plaque recorded the creation of the Garden of Remembrance as the Borough's War Memorial [fig. 7.19].[41] With an eye to easier maintenance, some chest tombs were disassembled, and many more tombstones were laid flat and gradually disappeared below grass.

Maintenance of the old churchyard, in particular the flower beds of the Garden of Remembrance, was now the responsibility of the local authority. But the tower remained a consecrated building with the bells still in use. A quotation was received in 1957 for running repairs to bells, but nothing was done. Two years later a report on the tower by A. R. Reed was made to the Society for the Protection of Ancient Buildings (SPAB). It noted some minor problems and recommended a new report on the bells.[42]

THE BELLS

The report on the bells made in 1959 by the Whitechapel Bell Foundry was alarming; there was excessive movement in the tower even when only one bell was rung, because the bells were too high up and the frame in poor condition. It seems likely that the demolition of the church in 1927 had reduced the stability of the heightened tower when the bells were swung. Suggestions that the bells be rehung lower down (cost £1,400) or fitted with a chiming apparatus (£100) were not pursued, and in 1961 the Foundry quoted £96 6s. for lowering the bells to the ground, recommending that the belfry – which was 'in a filthy state' – should be cleared out. It was decided that the bells no longer had a future in Hornsey; in 1964 the Foundry reported to the London Diocesan Fund on their transfer to St-George-in-the-East. This notable Stepney church by Nicholas Hawksmoor had been gutted in the war and had lost its bells; new bells were a fitting culmination to the work on the new church which was being completed within the shell of the old walls.[43] The Foundry, having recorded details of the old bells, recast them in a light peal of eight. With the loss of the bells, much mourned by the local ringers, the tower no longer had a useful function.

THE FATE OF THE VICTORIAN CHURCH

Problems for St Mary's were not confined to the old tower. By the later 1960s the dangerous state of the Victorian building was becoming increasingly evident. A detailed report prepared by the architect Cecil Brown in 1965 referred to 'the rocking movement of the structure and the tendency to disintegration and failure'. It examined the costs of underpinning and repair (£57,000); repair and partial demolition (£67,000); and total demolition and rebuilding (£54,000 or £63,000 depending on size).[44] The new Rector appointed in 1966, Philip Brassel, was appalled by what he found: 'Arches in the North shored up, more had to be supported in a year or so; the heating system which was dilapidated, became unworkable, several banks of lights were operated by removal or replacement of fuses as the wiring to switchboards became perished and live … A general sense of decay, cold, gloom and that the building was simply not safe, whatever the surveyors said, made its use as a place of living worship almost impossible, in spite of the great affection still held for it by many of its old adherents.'[45]

Further estimates for repair and partial demolition were prepared but in 1967 the Diocese determined on total demolition and rebuilding. The bureaucracy following this decision was considerable. An Act of Parliament was passed in 1969, stating procedures and conditions.[46] Plans for the new building had to be approved by the Diocesan Advisory Committee and the Borough, and the public notified, as it was a departure from the local development plan. A meeting attended by the Rector and F. G. Hippolite (from Biscoe & Stanton, surveyors to the Diocese), was held with the Borough's planning and education officers in October 1967, to consider the future of the site.[47] Hippolite's report stated that the Borough was keen to use part of it for a new Infant school; work would need to start before March 1969

7.20 Interior with scaffolding; the Brooks church in the 1960s (Hornsey Parish Church Archives)

105

in order to qualify for the finance available. The planning officer, David Frith, favoured a unified approach, with detailed plans for both school and church submitted before full consent was granted, so that a harmonious whole could be achieved. But what happened was rather different.

The demolition took place in 1969, leaving only the low decorative boundary walls along the High Street and Church Lane [fig. 7.21]. The Diocesan Advisory Committee sent a list of fittings and monuments worthy of preservation; these, including the organ, were initially stored at a neighbouring church, St Peter Wightman Road.[48] The congregation moved, as a temporary measure, to the parish hall on the north side of the High Street, taking with them the altarpiece from the War Memorial Chapel.[49] Demolition of churches, especially Victorian ones, was not uncommon in the 1950s–70s. Dozens of examples in Greater London disappeared during this period, some because rebuilding after war damage was not considered feasible, others because they stood in the way of radical building schemes. Victorian architecture was only just beginning to be taken seriously and very few Victorian churches had the protection of being listed buildings and qualifying for financial assistance. It was only during the 1970s that more positive and constructive attitudes to repair and conservation began to develop, together with appreciation of the merits of Victorian architects such as James Brooks.[50] While the congregation had an affection for the building, its dangerous condition, the dour appearance of the Brooks exterior and the unfinished tower in the setting of a depressed suburban High Street, did not arouse either local passion or artistic inspiration. The single exception is a photograph conveying the melancholy drama of the ruins [fig. 7.22].

7.21 Boundary wall of the Brooks church

7.22 The Brooks church under demolition (Hornsey Parish Church Archives)

PLANS FOR REBUILDING

A short brief for the new church was prepared by the rector and the PCC.[51] It was to be traditional in character (with altar and sanctuary at the east end) with seating for 250–350, and should include space for the Middlesex Regiment's Memorial Chapel and, if possible, incorporation of the old tower.[52] The novelty was the quantity of ancillary rooms demanded, including a hall which could be opened up to the church if required. The emphasis was on twentieth-century practicality, not grandeur, a smaller church with the additional social spaces that were increasingly required by contemporary places of worship. The hope of having a tower with bells was not forgotten, and in 1969 the architect, Cecil Brown, was in contact with the Whitechapel Bell Foundry, which offered to advise on how new bells might be hung in the old tower. Brown was a church architect working for the Diocese of London, best known for his careful post-war reconstruction of the interior of the Wren church of St Lawrence Jewry in the City. But his negotiations with the Haringey planners, which continued for over four years, became increasingly unsatisfactory.

No unified plan for church and school emerged. Plans for the Infant school on the site of the Victorian church were developed rapidly for the trustees of the school by the architects Laurence King & Partners. The new church therefore had to be sited in the old churchyard, which created a number of difficulties, not least the disturbance of burials and the threat to an open space valued for its mature trees. Both architect and planners had agreed early on that a vista should be maintained through the churchyard; the proposed plan therefore sited the church north to south (at right angles to the site of the old church), with a small chapel behind the altar for the war memorial, and parish rooms adjoining at the other end. Shallow-arched arcades were proposed as links to the school and the tower, anchoring the plain brick building in its setting. The proposals included car parking and the creation of a 'Garden of Rest' south of the arcade, in place of the Garden of Remembrance created twenty years earlier on the site of the old church. Brown's plan for the new church and parish rooms was submitted to the Council in June 1971 but was deferred for further discussion.[53] At the request of the planners a view by the artist Peter Saintsbury was prepared; the proposals were illustrated in the *Hornsey Journal* in November 1971 and in an exhibition in the Town Hall in December [fig. 7.23]. The church was shown as a plain brick structure; its north-facing, windowless 'east' end to the High Street embellished by a small canopied feature (a detail disliked by the planners). The entrance was in the side facing the old tower. The style was quietly modern, in the manner of some post-war buildings of the 1950s, with no Gothic reminiscences; the plan was traditional, with passage aisles, large windows along the east-facing wall and a step up to the sanctuary. More innovative was the proposal for the substantial two-storey octagonal building behind, intended as community rooms, with doors opening to the church and, on the floor above, a youth room and small flat.

The planners were not enthusiastic, regarding the proposed building as 'a rather uninspired and mediocre edifice', objecting especially to the dull elevations of the bulky community building.[54] Planning permission was given for the church on 31 December 1971, but subject to agreement on details of the halls and car park. The details submitted were rejected by the planners in June 1972.[55] Discussion dragged on for two years, until the church appealed against the planners' failure to resolve the matter. In order to avoid a public inquiry scheduled for February 1974, the plans, with a few minor changes, were finally agreed at

7.23 Perspective view by Peter Saintsbury, 1973, of the proposed church designed by Cecil Brown (Hornsey Parish Church Archives)

the last minute, at the request of the Development Control Panel.[56] In the end nothing was built. The key issue which emerges from the evidence available is that the planners' hope for a distinguished landmark was completely at variance with the approach of the architect. The vice-chair of the planning committee, Councillor Neil Cameron, was quoted as saying: 'Here was an opportunity to provide something architecturally outstanding – in a dominant position in the area.'[57] In contrast, Cecil Brown wrote in defence of his design: ' the vision of a church is not necessarily to express the age in which it is built, not to strike a note of novelty but to be a help to worship … Reticence in design goes … to produce an element of solemnity and inspires [a] sense of reverence…'[58] This basic difference was compounded by apparently contradictory advice from the planners, who, the church asserted, had failed to explain their objections and so made it impossible to resolve the issues, so that the church was unable to carry out the obligation to rebuild specified in the Act of Parliament.

Cecil Brown, exasperated by the alterations to his design, wrote to the rector on 6 March 1974, explaining that he wished to withdraw from the responsibility of building the church, though he offered to remain as consultant. The building was to have been funded by the sale of the land for the school.[59] However inflation during the 1970s made the building project increasingly unrealistic and in 1979 the decision was taken not to go ahead. Philip Brassel moved to a new post in Sussex and the congregation of St Mary's accepted with considerable reluctance that they should join with that of St George Cranley Gardens, a modern church of 1959, a mile away to the west.[60] The formal union took place in June 1982; St George was renamed St Mary with St George, and the Revd. Geoffrey Seabrook, the incumbent of St George since 1974, became the Rector of Hornsey.

A decision now had to be made about the fittings and monuments from St Mary's, most of which had been in store since 1969. In 1983 the small Baptistery at St George's was adapted to become the Regimental Memorial Chapel, housing the altarpiece which had been moved to the parish hall. The space was limited; the angels from the riddell posts were mounted on the wall and the additional war memorial boards to Hornsey parishioners were omitted.[61] The large slab to George Rey was set into the floor of a new parish room built the same year. The seventeenth century table, some other furniture and the parish chest were also brought to St George's.[62] It appears that a selection was made from the monuments; the brasses were remounted on stone slabs in 1984, and together with the memorials to past rectors were placed in the southwest corner of the church around the font, but were not given permanent fixed positions. The fate of other fittings and memorials recommended for preservation by the DAC is unknown, apart from the Francis Musters monument, which was acquired by the Victoria and Albert Museum in 2003.[63]

Had the church, halls and car park been built as intended, more of the internal monuments would probably have survived, but little would have remained of the southern part of the churchyard. Instead, the churchyard remained unaltered, although its remaining tombs suffered both from vandalism and from encroaching vegetation. The Garden of Remembrance, reprieved from

7.24 Walled up entrance to the tower, 1988

building proposals, was replanted by the Borough with low maintenance shrubs in place of bedding plants, but after this both the garden and the churchyard received little attention, apart from an annual tidy-up before the Remembrance Day ceremony. The disused tower suffered from several break-ins, following which the doors to the vestry and the basement were removed and all the openings, including the west window, were walled up [fig. 7.24].

---

[1] These figures refer to the parish of Hornsey when it included South Hornsey.

[2] On the development of Hornsey at this time see VCH, pp. 111-122; Janet Owen, *John Farrer: The Man who Changed Hornsey*, Hornsey Historical Society, 2009; *Lost Houses of Haringey*, Hornsey Historical Society, 1986.

[3] Lambeth Palace Library, ICBS 9211, St Mary Hornsey.

[4] Anthony Symondson, 'Theology, Worship and the Late Victorian Church', in *The Victorian Church: Architecture and Society*, ed. C. Brooks and A. Saint, Manchester University Press, 1995, pp. 192–222.

[5] *Hornsey Journal*, 2 June 1888.

[6] *St Mary Hornsey Parish Magazine*, July 1895, p. 3.

[7] Ibid., October 1889, December 1889.

[8] F. W. M. Draper, 'Hornsey Ringers' Jug', *Trans. London and Middlesex Archaeol. Soc.* n.s. X, 1951, p. 39.

[9] *St Mary Hornsey Parish Magazine*, May 1891, p. 4.

[10] LMA DRO20/B6/1/.

[11] *Report of Hornsey Urban District Council 1896–1900*, p. 31.

[12] C. J. M. Sidey, Churchwarden, *Notes on Hornsey Church and District*, Vol. I (Bruce Castle Museum).

[13] Sir Charles Nicholson, 'The Design and Arrangement of Churches', in *Recent Ecclesiastical Architecture*, Technical Journals Ltd, 1911.

[14] *St Mary Hornsey Parish Magazine*, October 1889, December 1889.

[15] For further details on the furnishings see C. J. M. Sidey (note 12 above).

[16] *VCH Middlesex*, vol. 6, p.173.

[17] The central figure of the Good Shepherd cost £25, the smaller statues £10 each. *St Mary Hornsey Parish Mazazine*, March and June 1907.

[18] See Chapter 3. Possibly of Dutch origin. Now at St Mary with St George.

[19] Nick Allaway, 'Hornsey in the First World War', *HHS Bulletin 44*, 2003, pp. 17–22.

[20] Hilda Sheppard, 'St Mary Hornsey', typescript in Hornsey Parish Church Archives.

[21] *Hornsey Journal*, 25 Jan 1929, p. 4.

[22] Sidey, Vol. I (see note 12).

[23] *Hornsey Journal*, 18 June 1926, p. 4.

[24] LMA B32/14; *Hornsey Journal*, 29 April 1927, p. 15.

109

[25] *Hornsey Journal*, 2 April 1929.

[26] *Hornsey Journal*, 6 May 1927, p. 15.

[27] The names are: Charles Rogers, Thomas Price, Richard D. Marshall, John Rogers, George Crawley, Frederick James Gant, Richard Clay, Benjamin Hands.

[28] Whitechapel Bell Foundry records, information kindly supplied by Revd. David L. Cawley.

[29] C. J. M. Sidey, Vol. V (see note 12).

[30] The upper part of the Towers monument survived in a battered state and is now in the tower basement. See Chapter 4.

[31] Mr Peter Campbell was thanked specially for his concern with the monuments. See *Hornsey Journal*, 22 April 1927, p. 12; 29 April 1927, p. 16.

[32] Photographs were taken by the Royal Commission on Historical Monuments in 1968. A record was made of the older monuments in the Royal Commission's *Middlesex* volume, published in 1935 (at this time the Commission's remit was restricted to items older than 1714).

[33] RCHM, *Middlesex*, 1935 p. 78.

[34] See Chapter 6 note 5.

[35] Correspondence, 3 November 1947, Hornsey Parish Church Archives.

[36] Sheppard, note 21 above. The author of the booklet was not named but was known to be the respected local historian F. W. M. Draper.

[37] Frederick Cleary (1905–84) was Chairman of the Plans and Town Planning Committee. The Hornsey scheme was the start of Cleary's lifelong campaign to make gardens and improve the environment. Cleary became Chairman of the Metropolitan Gardens Association, founded Haslemere Estates to restore historic buildings, and established several foundations to promote environmental education. His work to increase open space in the City of London was marked in 1982 by the creation of Cleary Gardens on Huggin Hill.

[38] *Hornsey Journal*, 8 April 1948.

[39] Hugh Casson et al., *Bombed Churches as War Memorials*, The Architectural Press, 1945.

[40] The design of the garden was not ideal for ceremonies with a large numbers of spectators, as the paths provided inadequate space for the public. On later occasions the numerous civilian wreath-layers approached from the south and had to walk over temporary paving slabs laid over the flower beds.

[41] The plaque has been repositioned on the remnant of the west wall north of the tower.

[42] Bruce Castle Museum, St Mary Hornsey. The SPAB report noted that the structural condition of the tower was good apart from a few small cracks of no significance. There was a vertical crack in the turret stair and some fall of stones from the turret parapet; the lead roof dated from 1833. It proposed removal of the weathervane, installation of a new drainpipe and repair of the top of turret. The weathervane was removed; it is unclear whether other repairs were carried out.

[43] Whitechapel Bell Company records, information kindly supplied by Revd. David L Cawley. The new peal weighed 29.5 cwt, the old peal 52.5 cwt.

[44] Hornsey Parish Church Archives: Report, 1965.

[45] Hornsey Parish Church Archives: Brief to the architect from the Rector and the PCC [1969].

[46] The St Mary Hornsey Act of 1969 stated that the medieval tower was to be maintained in situ by the PCC; the incumbent could demolish the existing building and sell or dispose of material, provided memorial stones, plaques etc. were preserved, installed or dealt with. A new church was to be completed in three years; no licence or faculty was needed and scheduled land might be sold.

[47] Hornsey Parish Church Archives: Letter from F. G. Hippolite to Revd. P. E. Brassel, 1 November 1967. From 1966 Hornsey was part of the London Borough of Haringey.

[48] Hornsey Parish Church Archives: the DAC's recommendations included all the fittings and monuments mentioned on pp. 97-8 and, in addition, the parish chest in the vestry, the long kneelers in the front pews 'which could be of use in another church', and the hanging cross referred to as the 'Montgomery-Campbell Rood'.

[49] The hall, built as a 'National Hall' in the late nineteenth century, was acquired by the parish in 1916.

[50] *Chapels and Churches: Who Cares?* by Marcus Binney and Peter Burman and the same authors' *Change and Decay: The Future of Our Churches*, 1977. *Change and Decay* lists dozens of losses in Greater London, (including three Victorian churches in Tottenham demolished in the early 1970s). (Erroneously it states that St Mary Hornsey was demolished and replaced.) Appreciation of James Brooks was pioneered by the research of Roger Dixon, co-author (with Stefan Muthesius) of *Victorian Architecture* (1978).

[51] Typescript in Hornsey Parish Church Archives.

[52] The brief mentioned provision for the organ, vestry and workroom, two parish rooms with modern facilities, one opening into the nave, and possibly some accommodation for curate or caretaker.

[53] Haringey Council Minutes 1971–72, p. 204, application No.1204/001/6.

[54] Haringey Council planning files 1204/001/6.

[55] Haringey Council Minutes 1971–72, p. 235, application no.1204/001/6.

[56] Planning permission was granted on 30 January 1974, after some minor alterations to the drawings previously submitted, chiefly concerning the form of the windows to the community rooms. Haringey Council Minutes 1973–74, p. 614.

[57] *Hornsey Journal*, 18 January 1974, p. 6.

[58] Hornsey Parish Church Archives, appeal papers 1974. The appeal includes a Proof of Evidence by the Rector, P. E. Brassel, and a statement by the senior planning officer. There is also a statement by the Rector on dealings with the planning officers 1969–71.

[59] Brassel, Proof of Evidence.

[60] St George Cranley Gardens was built to replace the church in Priory Road destroyed in the war.

[61] These boards were later discovered in a skip. They are now in the old tower.

[62] Thyrza Meacock, *A Hundred Year History of St George's Church Hornsey*, Hornsey Historical Society, 2006, pp. 61ff. Parish documents were transferred to the London Metropolitan Archives.

[63] There were reports that the store was not secure and had been broken into. The Musters monument was known to be on the market in the 1970s. It was acquired by the V and A in 2003 for £75,000 from C. A. and J. E. Finch, with the help of the Art Fund, which contributed £37,500. www.artfund.org. Visited October 2014. The loss of both the Candish obelisk and the column (but not the base) of the Atterbury monument suggest deliberate removal of pieces of architectural value. No comprehensive list of the monuments in the church is known; the only record appears to be the photographs taken for the National Monuments Record in 1968 before the monuments were removed from the church.

8.1 The basement entrance opened up   8.2 The damaged roof before repair

CHAPTER 8

An Old Site with a Future?

Towards the end of the twentieth century the neglected churchyard and its deserted ancient building gradually attracted more positive interest. In 1987 the North Middlesex Family History Society carried out an impressively thorough survey of the visible tombstones, recording the names on 172 graves in the main churchyard and 75 in the south extension, a notable contrast with the Borough Engineer's Plan of 1950 which had shown 326 graves in the old churchyard alone before the alterations for the garden.[1]

From 1980 Hornsey High Street had been designated as a Conservation Area. Concern grew among members of its Advisory Committee over the condition of the tower, the area's most important architectural monument and the oldest listed building in Hornsey, which had been added to English Heritage's Buildings at Risk Register. The committee was unclear about the ownership and responsibility for the building. As there was no means of gaining access, in 1987 committee members forced an entrance to investigate further, and discovered, alarmingly, that owing to theft of lead from the roof, timbers had rotted and the entire roof was in danger of collapse [figs. 8.1, 8.2]. The whole building was knee deep in pigeon detritus, and suffering from extreme damp. The conservation committee joined forces with the Hornsey Historical Society, and made contact with the Rector of Hornsey, Geoffrey Seabrook. This led to the formation of the 'St Mary's Hornsey Tower Committee'. Meetings were held at St Mary with St George, chaired by the Rector. The Rector favoured the use of the tower as an educational resource centre, but it was made clear that the Parochial Church Council of St Mary with St George would be unable and unprepared to fund the maintenance of the tower or finance its use.[2] At the meeting of 20 April 1989 it was agreed to establish the Friends of Hornsey Church Tower as a charitable body, with Joan Schwitzer as Chair, Hilda Johnston as Secretary, and current members of the St Mary's Tower Committee.[3]

The first meeting of the new group (FoHCT) was held on 15 May 1989, and Anthony Richardson was invited to join as advisory architect.[4] A constitution was drawn up and adopted and registration as a charity was achieved in January 1990; supporters were invited to join, with a £5 annual membership fee. Funds from a number of sources made it possible to carry out emergency repairs in 1988–89, creating secure entrances to both the basement and the vestry, clearing out rubbish, screening the windows against pigeons and installing a new beam to support the roof (there was much excitement when this was delivered by a large crane) [fig. 8.3].[5] On the first, very successful, Open Day, 8 October 1989, visitors were able to climb up to the ringing chamber, a second Open Day taking place the following year. On 30 June 1991 it was possible to provide access to the roof. It was clear from the reactions of visitors that many had no idea of the original function of the building, but there was much enthusiasm for climbing the tower and enjoying the views [fig. 8.4]. By then a new roof surface of paving slabs had been laid by Friends' volunteers, together with steel safety railings around the parapets (the materials were hauled up by hand pulley, rope and basket, in medieval fashion, in pouring rain). A Friends' newsletter was inaugurated in Spring 1991; possible new uses for the building were discussed, as museum, chapel, meeting room, teaching space and viewing platform. The Friends published small booklets about the history of the tower, the lost church and the churchyard.[6] There were efforts to interest the local schools, and a number of visits organised, but further development of the tower as an educational centre foundered over the difficulties of providing necessary facilities. Later publicity away from the site included an exhibition of historic artists' views, held at the Old Schoolhouse, and another, held at St Mary with St George, which focused on the interest of the surviving monuments now in the church at Cranley Gardens [see fig. 3.1].[7]

The Friends developed a yearly routine with a number of fundraising activities. From 1995 these included an annual 'Towers and Turrets' coach tour to churches of interest (especially those with towers to climb), which proved very popular, and the summer Open Day became famous for the 'Teddy abseiling' from the top of the tower [fig. 8.5]. Further work on the tower was carried out as funds allowed. In 1996 repairs included the vestry ceiling, with its decorative plaster ribs and bosses; in 2000-01 the opening up of the blocked west window, at a cost of £3,000, transformed the former vestry into a cheerful well-lit space [fig. 8.8]. The wooden War Memorial boards from the church, which had been discovered in a skip (see above p. 98) were presented to the FoHCT, given a new frame, and hung on the north wall in 2003 [fig. 8.7]. The repairs made it possible for St Mary with St George to make regular use of the building. With funding from the PCC the vestry room was furnished as a chapel and from 2004 Sunday church services and Wednesday children's meetings were initiated as part of the church's 'Look East' project, which focused on the eastern part of the parish.[8]

8.3 Delivery of the new roof beam, 1991 8.4 Visitors on the roof, 2006 8.5 Teddy abseiling, 2006
8.6 The vestry room during repair, 1996 8.7 War Memorial boards to Hornsey parishioners, re-erected in the tower 2003
8.8 The vestry interior refurnished as a chapel, in use from 2004

8.4

8.8

8.7

8.5

8.3

8.6

8.13

8.14

8.11

The room also proved a successful venue for small concerts, cultural activities and meetings organised by the FoHCT, and for refreshments after the annual outdoor carol service.

It was clear, though, that the exterior of the tower required major attention, including repointing, replacement of missing stones and securing the battlements. Major funding made this possible in 2005-06.[9] The tower was scaffolded and suitable replacement stone was found to enable sensitive conservation of the external stonework [fig. 8.9].[10] Repair and regilding of the eighteenth-century clock face on the west wall made a strong impact (although persuading the clock to keep time was a continuing struggle) [fig. 8.10]. Additional funding from the Heritage of London Trust enabled conservation work on the external angel carvings. Further work on the interior in 2011 included the replacement of the lost ceiling to the ringing chamber, using recycled timber [fig. 8.11].

THE CHURCHYARD

In 1989 the maintenance of the churchyard by Haringey Council had been considered satisfactory, if uninspiring.[11] But during the 1990s the situation deteriorated. The Garden of Remembrance was full of straggling unkempt bushes; ash and elder seedlings were thrusting through collapsed chest tombs; rusty street lamps, no longer working, added to the sense of neglect, as did the quantity of litter and dumped rubbish. The broken-down seats in the Garden of Remembrance were occupied by drinkers, discouraging other visitors. It became clear that repairing the tower was not enough, it was essential to make the churchyard a more inviting place. The Friends carried out regular litter-picking and waged a wearying but eventually successful battle with the Council over the installation (and then the emptying) of litter bins. The broken seats were removed, ecologically-friendly compost bins were installed and more sensitive pruning of the bushes by the Friends replaced the Council's annual brutal trim and use of weedkiller. From 2003 the Friends held regular 'gardening days' and gradually a good relationship with the parks department was achieved, with the Council clearing away the mountains of debris created and returning it as mulch for the flower beds [fig. 8.12].[12] It was necessary to reconcile sometimes conflicting priorities: encouraging habitats for wild life; respecting the appeal of a romantically wild area; creating a safe and secure space for visitors; and maintaining the monuments [fig. 8.13].

The FoHCT's policy of recapturing something of the old rural character of the area led in 2003 to the replacement of the privet hedge along the High Street by a mixed hedge including hawthorn, hazel and rose, work carried out with the help of the British Trust for Conservation Volunteers. Further activities to encourage biodiversity and strengthen the value of the churchyard as part of a 'green chain' through Hornsey included bluebell planting in the 'woodland' of the south-east corner, and apple trees in 2010 close to the school entrance, which had been railed off earlier to provide a 'dog free area'. Elsewhere, other trees were planted as personal memorials [fig. 8.14].[13] A survey of plant life was

8.9 Repair of the battlements, 2009 8.10 The western clock face after conservation
8.11 Reinstatement of the ringing chamber ceiling, 2011 8.12 Welcome assistance from the Council lorry
8.13 The wild churchyard maintained 8.14 Planting of a tree in memory of Joan Schwitzer, 2010

8.21

8.22

PAST, PRESENT AND FUTURE

The FoHCT began with the aim of rescuing an historical monument from imminent dereliction. In response to conservation thinking in the 1990s, the intention was also to give the tower a useful function, which it had lost when the bells were removed. At the time of writing, after nearly fifty years of uncertainty, the tower is once again a focus for worship, not as in the past, as an adjunct to the larger adjoining space of the parish church, but as a distinct entity in its own right. Its worked-over fabric retains intriguing clues to its history through five hundred years [fig. 8.23]. Modern floodlighting and improvements to its setting have helped recover its identity as a valued local landmark in the High Street and a focus for community activities. Participation in London Open House weekends attracts visitors from further afield. The tower no longer defines a rural village; instead it provides a vantage point from which to survey Hornsey's position in the wider metropolitan landscape.

Care of the churchyard and its memorials was a natural further development; improved maintenance achieved through active community involvement, with increased support from Haringey Council, transformed the site into a peaceful green space which can be enjoyed by all [fig. 8.24]. Over the last twenty-five years the educational and cultural potential of the site as a whole has been demonstrated by a wide variety of activities: training in the use of lime mortar for repair of historic buildings; the use of the tower as a film location and a subject for photographic students; and in 2015 as a drama centre for the Crouch End Festival. Gardening activities attracted a band of keen volunteers, inspiring two of them to pursue careers in horticulture. The churchyard has benefited from the planting of seeds and bulbs by school children, and has inspired creativity in 'green art' sessions. Community events have included open days, picnics, concerts and firework watching from the top of the tower. The monuments, both those in the churchyard and those from the church which are preserved elsewhere, are recognised as a historical resource which is valued not only by social historians but is of interest to genealogists, art historians and geologists.

The tower and churchyard survive owing to an arbitrary combination of factors: the force of official protection of ancient buildings and historic sites; the generally conservative approach of the Anglican Church to consecrated ground; the loyalty of the former congregation to the old site, and efforts of many people over the last quarter-century in giving new life to both tower and churchyard. The unstable foundations of the Victorian church and lack of funds for rebuilding also played a part. So too did the romantic antiquarianism of the nineteenth century when the 'ivy-mantled tower' became a symbol of a lost village engulfed in suburban London. Today the ivy has gone, but the tower in its leafy churchyard remains for future generations.

8.20 A tribute from Dutch television on Gerard van Linde's tomb, 2010
8.21 Green Art on Jacob Walker's tomb, 2009 8.22 Work on the tomb survey, 2011
8.23 Pets' service 2013 8.24 A green churchyard to be enjoyed by all

[1] *Monumental Inscriptions with Index, St Mary Hornsey*, recorded by Pauline Dallman, Enid Hunt and friends, North Middlesex Family History Society, 1987. Typescript (copy with Hornsey Historical Society).

[2] Minutes of St Mary Hornsey Tower Committee 20 April 1989. At this point the responsibilities of the Rector and PCC were unclear. It was subsequently established from the St Mary Hornsey Act of 1969 that the incumbent Rector was the sole owner of both tower and churchyard, and therefore responsible for the upkeep of the tower. Maintenance of the 'closed churchyard' was the responsibility of the local authority.

[3] The 1969 St Mary Hornsey Act laid the responsibility for maintenance of the tower on the PCC. However, the Diocese of London noted in a letter to the FoHCT dated 13 June 1989 that the Edmonton Pastoral Committee had agreed in principle that the FoHCT should take over responsibility for the use, care and maintenance of the tower either through the issue of a licence under faculty or through a Pastoral Scheme. At the FoHCT meeting on 17 July 1989 it was noted that with the former method the care and responsibility for the tower would remain with the PCC, but that the PCC could delegate this to the FoHCT who would then take on responsibility under a lease. The alternative Pastoral Scheme would involve redundancy and take much longer to implement but would allow the Diocesan authorities to sell the tower if they were so minded. A decision was made by the church in September 1989 to apply for a faculty licence to empower the FoHCT to be appointed as lessees rather than seek redundancy. One reason given for this was that there was no wish to relinquish ownership of the tower as it had strong associations with parishioners of St Mary with St George. The church recognised that, although they had legal responsibility under the 1969 St Mary Hornsey Act for maintenance of the tower, this was well beyond parish means. They proposed that a Trust should be set up by FoHCT as a limited company to take on a lease to assume this responsibility. This issue was eventually resolved, with final responsibility for maintenance of the tower remaining with the Rector of Hornsey and, with his consent, the FoHCT acting as agent to assist in respect of maintenance, repair and improvement works to the tower, churchyard and Garden of Remembrance.

[4] FoHCT Minute book. In 1992 Peter Sanders took over as Chair, with Bridget Cherry as Secretary (both were also members of the Conservation Area Committee). Ken Gay became Treasurer, Newsletter editor and Membership secretary. In a few years the membership reached 100. The Hornsey Historical Society provided valuable support and publicity, and those who joined the Friends included many HHS members. Some supporters lived close to the site, others elsewhere in Haringey and a few even further afield. A special attraction was the opportunity for practical do-it-yourself maintenance of both tower and churchyard, undertaken by a core of dedicated volunteers, supported by many others on Open Days.

[5] FoHCT Minute book. In May 1989 £9,388 had been raised: £3,256.50 from an English Heritage London grant, £2,941 from Haringey, £1,000 from the British Legion, over £2,000 from other donors, including the Heritage of London Trust.

[6] Five booklets were published by FoHCT in 1990: Ian Murray, *St Mary's Church Hornsey*; Bridget Cherry, *Hornsey Church Tower: A Brief History and Guide*; David Bevan, *Hornsey Churchyard Nature Trail*; Joan Schwitzer, *An Introduction to St Mary's Hornsey Churchyard: Ten Notable Victorians and Their Families*; Eric Robinson, *St Mary's Tombstone Trail*. New editions of the last two were published in 2000 by the HHS under the titles: *Buried in Hornsey: The Graves of St Mary's Churchyard*, and *Geology from a Churchyard: A Tombstone Trail Round St Mary's, Hornsey*.

[7] *Hornsey Church Depicted*, at the Old Schoolhouse, 2008 (see HHS Bulletin 49, 2008, pp.36–9); *Explore the Past, Enrich the Future* at St Mary with St George, 2009, both curated by Frances Colquhoun and Bridget Cherry.

[8] Services were discontinued during later building work, but were re-established in 2013.

[9] Funding to a total of £18,000 came from a Joint English Heritage and Heritage Lottery Fund churches grant (the tower being eligible as it was now regularly used for worship) with partnership funding from the FoHCT, St Mary with St George, and 'section 106 money' from the Borough of Haringey (amenity improvement in connection with the development of the nearby Waterworks site). The case for repair was strengthened by the raising of the listing status of the tower to Grade 2*.

[10] Decayed Reigate stone was replaced by stone from Chicksgrove, Wilts; the dark 'ferricrete' by stone from Westerham, Kent. The work was carried out for Anthony Richardson Architects by Cliveden Conservation.

[11] FoHCT minutes 18 August 1989.

[12] A major drawback was that maintenance of the churchyard came under the highways department; more sympathetic and appropriate cooperation with the parks department was achieved only gradually.

[13] A Wild Cherry in memory of Joan Schwitzer, 2010; a Magnolia Stellata in memory of Alan Fox, a long term member of the Friends, 2012, a Mountain Ash in memory of Revd. Geoffrey Seabrook, 2013.

[14] These works were funded with help from the Heritage of London Trust and the Borough of Haringey Highways Department.

[15] The work was carried out from 2009–12 and 214 items were recorded, roughly 86% of the monuments recorded in 1987. Losses included stones which had disappeared when a new school boundary fence was built to the east, encroaching on part of the churchyard. Of the surviving gravestones, 20% could be dated from before 1800, 20% from 1800–1840, and 25% post-1840. 35% were undatable, with no legible inscription. Copies of the Tomb Survey and the Management Plan are deposited with the HHS at the Old Schoolhouse, and summaries are available on the FoHCT website.

PHOTO ALBUM 2005-14

1) Highgate Wood School visit, 2009. 2) Green Art, 2009. 3) Celebrating the first award of the Green Pennant, 2010. 4) Carol Service, December 2014. 5) Architect Anthony Richardson on the scaffolding, 2005. 6) Summer view with meadow grass, 2009. 7) Work on the Garden of Remembrance, 2013. 8) Father Geoffrey Seabrook arriving on Open Day, 2006. 9) Father Bruce Batstone at the Pets' Service, 2012. 10) Winter view from the north, 2010. 11) Winter view from the south, 2009. 12) Chairman Peter Sanders with the broken urn discovered near the Pattinson tomb, 2009. 13) Hornsey Festival, 2014. 14) Churchyard tour: studying the tower, 2009. 15) In the Garden of Remembrance, 2014. 16) Concert by the Byrdsong Choir, 2012. 17) Chest tombs, summer 2009.

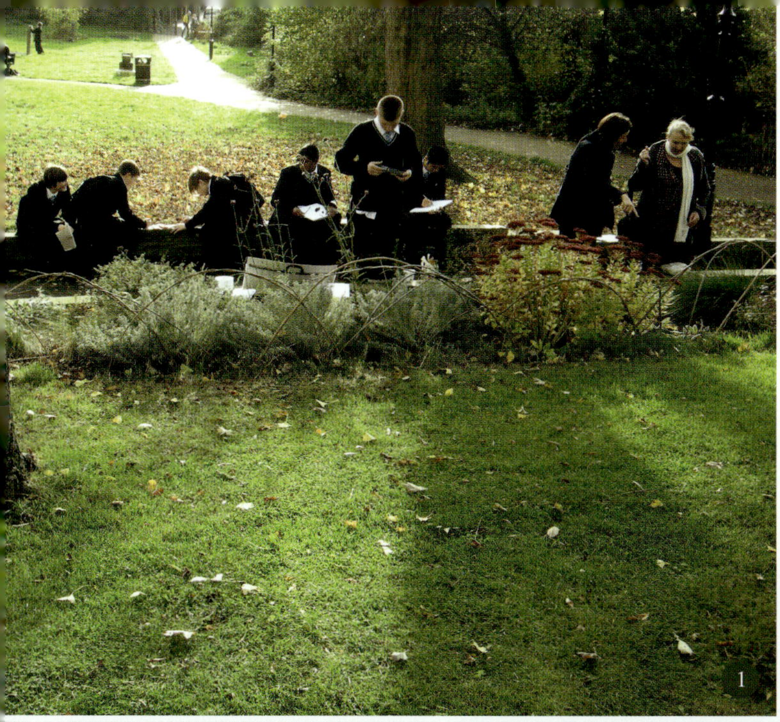
1

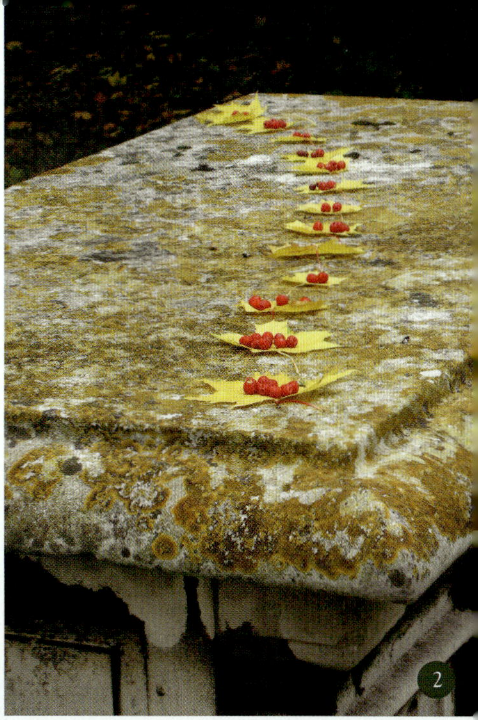
2

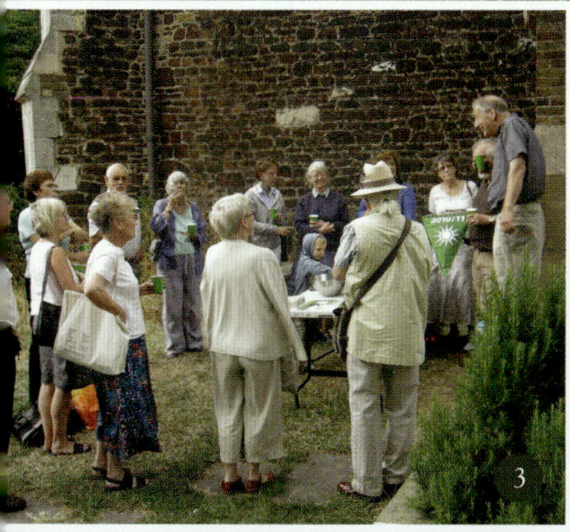
3

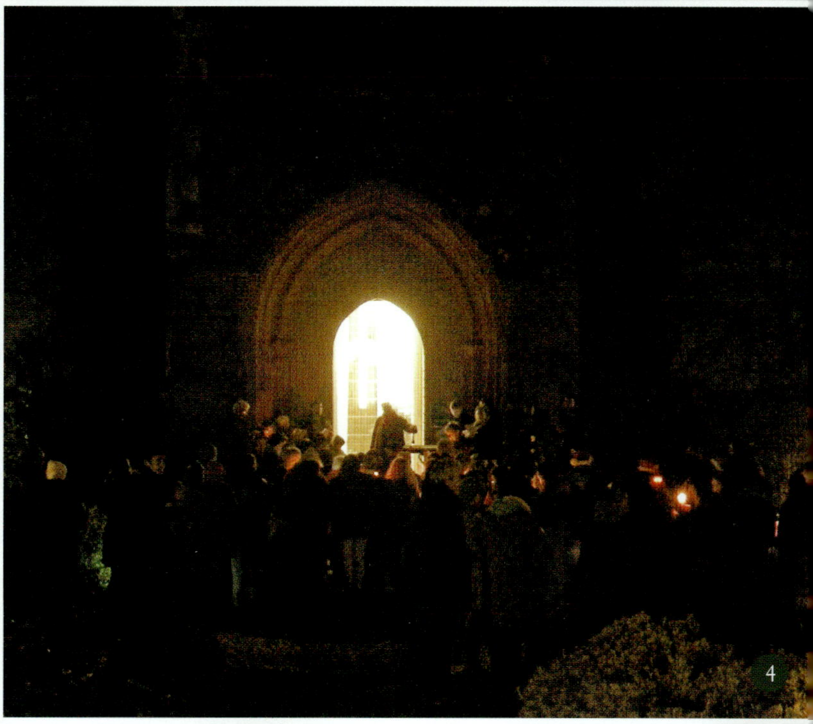
4

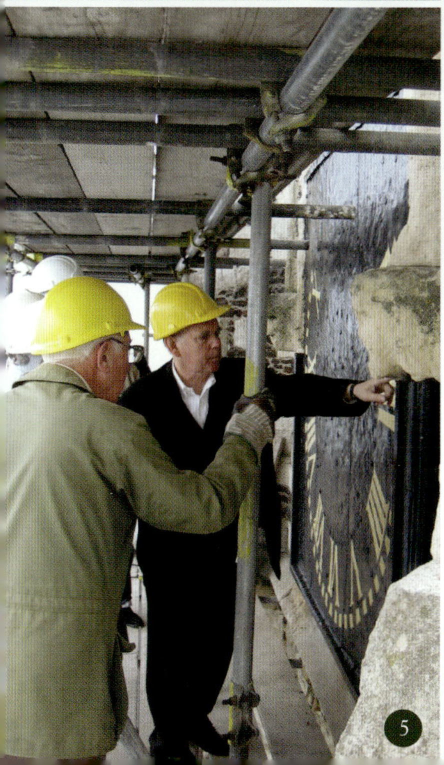
5

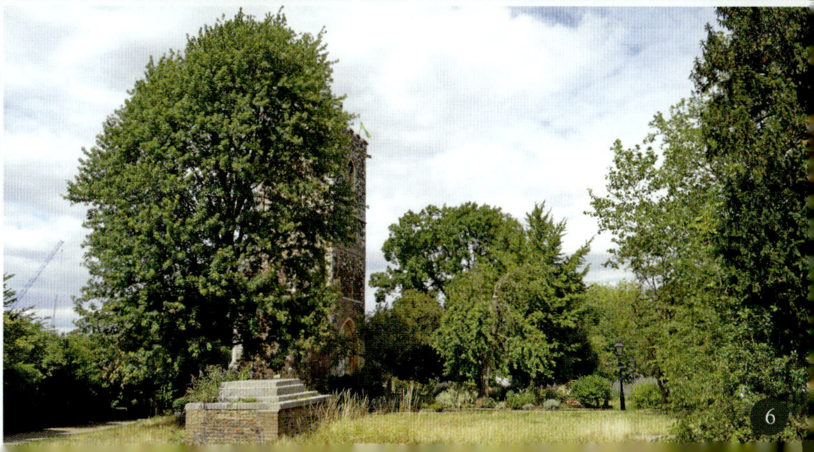
6

7

11

15

9

10

13

14

16

17

The churchyard ecology: trees and plants

The plant list compiled by David Bevan in 2010 identified over 150 plants and trees. They testify to the significance of the churchyard as a valuable open space for wild life, offering a variety of habitats ranging from woodland and open meadow, around the more formal arrangement of the Garden of Remembrance. In order to maintain variety and to encourage biodiversity the management plan divided the churchyard into separate zones, each requiring different treatment. The open grass areas, chiefly in the south extension and near the High Street hedge, are cut annually, to allow wild flowers to set seed, in contrast to the more frequently cut grass of the Garden of Remembrance. The undergrowth and smaller trees in the western border are allowed to grow up, but with some tactful intervention to make some of the tombs accessible.

The variety of trees is noteworthy, giving interest to the churchyard at all times of year. In the western border there are Elm suckers; they grow only to a limited height before dying back, but are likely to be descendants of the elm trees visible in eighteenth century views. The Hawthorns could have descended from the quickthorn hedge which once surrounded the churchyard. The woodland area on the fringe of the south extension must have been open land when first included in the churchyard in 1839. Among the trees that have grown up since are numerous Hornbeams, a tree native to Middlesex. The western border harbours Mountain Ash, Service Tree, Elder and Crab Apple. Other substantial trees include Oak, Ash, (a very large specimen north of the Garden), London Plane, Norway Maple, Field Maple and Lime. There are the churchyard favourites of Yew and Holly, the latter probably planted in the nineteenth century along the path to the north door of the church. More recent plantings include the two large Ginkgo trees in the Garden of Remembrance, Apple trees in the railed area near the eastern border, and several memorial trees (Wild Cherry, Mountain Ash, Magnolia Stellata) have been planted since 2000. The wild flowers are similarly diverse, ranging from native bluebells and wood anemones in the woodland, to celandines in the borders and meadow flowers in the open areas.

Opposite: autumn view of the Tower and Garden of Remembrance; Norway Maple in centre, Ginkgo on extreme right, contrasted with Holly (left) and Yew (in background).

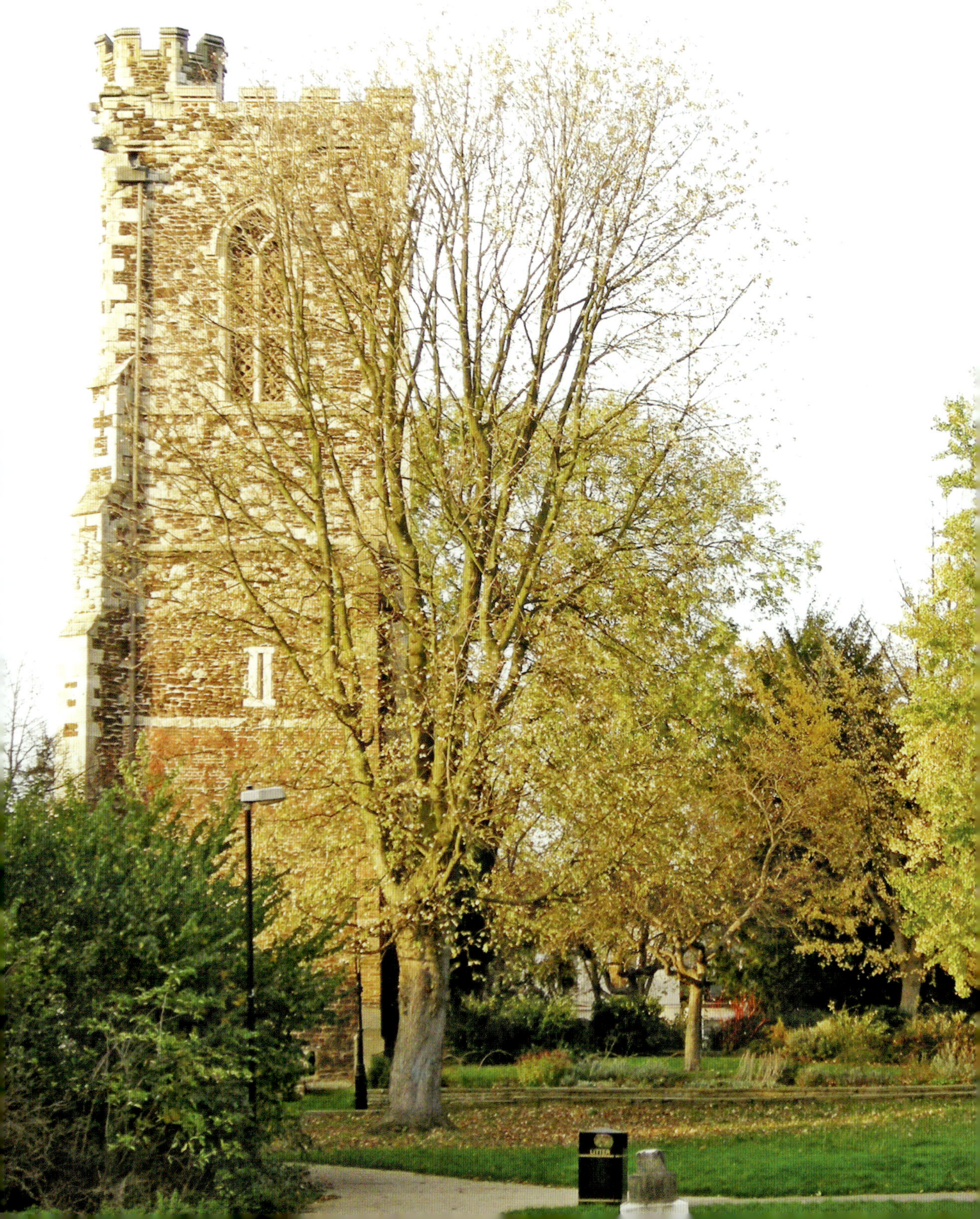

ST MARY'S HORNSEY CHURCHYARD
Locations of monuments & other features mentioned in the text

1. Lady Basset Ledger
2. Garden of Remembrance
3. 18th Century Headstones
4. Holly Trees
5. William Poulton Headstone
6. High Street Hedge
7. Morgan Family, James Weedon & Clarke Family Chest Tombs
8. Rogers Family Chest Tomb
9. Ware Family Monument
10. Eastern Boundary
11. Revd. Geoffrey Seabrook's Memorial Mountain Ash Tree
12. Ginkgo Trees
13. William Pattinson Chest Tomb
14. Apple Trees
15. Joan Schwitzer's Memorial Wild Cherry Tree
16. Alan Fox's Memorial Magnolia Stellata
17. Mitchell Family Chest Tomb
18. Southern Extension of Churchyard
19. Harriet Long and Jacob Walker Tomb
20. Joshua Toulmin Smith Tomb
21. Peacock & Block Family Tombs* and Peacock Daughters Tomb**
22. Gerard van de Linde Tomb
23. Revd. William Snell Low Coped Tomb Chest
24. Smith Family Chest Tomb
25. Judith Suley Standing Headstone
26. Henry Pott Standing Headstone
27. Robert Carter & Joseph Seaton Headstones
28. Henry Warner Vault

This plan is based on a digital survey carried out by Randall Surveys in 1997
Updating and adaptation by Peter Sanders in 2015

LOCATION OF MONUMENTS AND OTHER FEATURES MENTIONED IN THE TEXT

1. Lady Basset of Trehidy, Cornwall, 1682. The most notable among the group of ledgers from the church relocated in the Garden of Remembrance.
2. Garden of Remembrance. Laid out as a war memorial in 1950 on the site of the old church. Two Ginkgo trees may date from the 1950s. Borders replanted by FoHCT 2008-12. Magnolia Stellata in the centre planted in memory of Alan Fox, 2012. The lamp posts along the surrounding paths were replaced in 2013.
3. Six headstones north of the tower dating from 1750-1815.
4. Holly trees north of the tower, formerly lining a path to the south door of the church rebuilt in 1833 (now marked by a metal arch in the Garden of Remembrance).
5. William Poulton, 1888. Red granite headstone.
6. High Street hedge. Replanted with mixed species, 2003.
7. Surviving chest tombs north of the church. From west to east: Morgan family, from Bridge End in Glamorgan, mid-eighteenth century; James Weeding, died 1817; Clarke family from Lincolns Inn, Holborn.
8. Samuel Rogers, died 1855. Rogers family chest tomb, 1832. Raised tomb with iron railings, repaired 2000. (Listed Grade II)
9. Ware family monument, early nineteenth century. Low horizontal sandstone slab.
10. Eastern boundary with Infant School.
11. Mountain Ash planted in memory of Revd. Geoffrey Seabrook, 2014.
12. Ginkgo trees.
13. William Pattinson, 1844. Chest tomb; the urn formerly on top is now in the tower basement.
14. Apple trees planted 2010.
15. Wild Cherry tree planted in memory of Joan Schwitzer, 2010.
16. Magnolia Stellata planted in memory of Alan Fox.
17. Mitchell family tomb, in use 1796-1846. Raised chest tomb.
18. Southern extension of the churchyard, in use from 1839.
19. Harriet Long and her servant Jacob Walker, 1840. Listed Grade II in 2009 in recognition of its special interest in relation to emancipation.
20. Joshua Toulmin Smith, 1869.
21. Block family, of The Grove Muswell Hill, and Peacock family of Southwood, Highgate. Substantial granite tombs of the 1860s.
22. Gerard van der Linde, 1858. Plain slab. Dutch poet known as 'The Schoolmaster'.
23. Revd. William Snell, 1854; low coped tomb chest with Gothic ornament.
24. Smith family tomb chest, eighteenth century.
25. Judith Suley, died 1712. The oldest surviving standing tomb in the churchyard.
26. Henry Pott, 1816, sandstone headstone.
27. In the tower basement: Robert Carter, 1689, and Joseph Seaton, 1693, headstones moved from the churchyard; Hannah Towers 1753, upper part of a monument formerly within the church.
28. Vault for Henry Warner, created when the church was rebuilt, 1833.

For further details on some individual tombs see Joan Schwitzer, *Buried in Hornsey*, HHS, 2000, and information on the FoHCT website: www.hornseychurchtower.com

A BRIEF OVERVIEW OF PRINCIPAL ARCHIVAL SOURCES CONSULTED

Abbreviations used in the end notes:

BC *Bruce Castle Museum*

BL *British Library*

BM *British Museum*

FoHCT *Friends of Hornsey Church Tower*

HHS *Hornsey Historical Society*

ICBS *Incorporated Church Building Society*

LMA *London Metropolitan Archives*

NMR *National Monuments Record, Historic England*

ODNB *Oxford Dictionary of National Biography*

TNA *The National Archive*

VCH *Victoria County History Middlesex, vol. VI*

The most useful general introduction to the history of the church and the parish is in the *Victoria County History of Middlesex*, volume VI 1980. The written records for St Mary Hornsey are scattered and incomplete; the emphasis of the different chapters of this book reflects the character of the often limited sources available. The London Metropolitan Archives holds London Commissary Court records of medieval wills of Hornsey parishioners (formerly in the City of London Guildhall Collections, 9171). The inventory of the church made in 1552 is at The National Archive (TNA E 315/498). The LMA also holds the parish records from the seventeenth century up to the nineteenth century (including baptismal, marriage and burial registers, and Vestry minutes, although these are patchy for the period before 1800). The notes of the eighteenth century antiquary William Cole are at the British Library (Add MSS 5836); the records of the Incorporated Church Building Society, relating to the building work of 1833 and 1888, are at Lambeth Palace Library. Bruce Castle Museum (Haringey Culture Library and Learning), has a Vestry minute book of the nineteenth century and various miscellaneous papers, including the early twentieth century notes of churchwarden C.J.M. Sidey. The Hornsey Historical Society has parish magazines of the earlier twentieth century, some miscellaneous correspondence, and early photographs; it also holds copies of the survey of monuments made by the North Middlesex Family History Society and the Tomb Condition Survey made by FoHCT. A particularly valuable treasure trove is the Potter Collection in the Department of Prints and Drawings, British Museum (mostly available online), whose material relating to Highgate and Hornsey collected in the late nineteenth century includes both cuttings and illustrations.

Both Bruce Castle and the LMA have important collections of paintings, drawings and prints (the LMA collection, formerly at Guildhall, is available on line at collage.cityoflondon.gov.uk). The National Monuments Record, Historic England, has a photographic record of the Victorian church and its contents before its demolition in 1968. Hornsey Parish Church, St Mary with St George, Cranley Gardens, holds archives relating to the demolition and proposed rebuilding of St Mary's in the 1960s-70s. The records of the Friends of Horney Church Tower (c/o Hornsey Historical Society) cover the last twenty five years, further information on their work can be found on their website www.hornseychurchtower.com

INDEX

A
Alforth, William 32
Angier, Elizabeth and Burrage 53, 54
Anthony Richardson Architects 120n10
Armitage, Samuel 40
Arnald, George, frontispiece .. 17, *17*, 18, 19, 24, 25, 61
Art Fund 110n63
Atterbury, Lewis (Rector) 50, 50, 59n, 78, 110n63

B
Bachelor, Henry 62, 63, 79
Bage, Mr. 74n10
Barnes, John, jun. 46n45
Barnet, Frances 42
Barnet, Rachel 42
Basse, Thomas 28, 32
Basset, Lady, of Tewidy 45, 101, 126-7
Basset, Sir Francis 45
Batstone, Bruce (Rector) 123
Behnes William, ... 78
Bendy, Samuel 41
Bevan, David 116, 124
Bewick, John 13
Bewick, Thomas 13
Biscoe and Stanton 105
Black, Anthony 42
Block, Elizabeth 88, 126-7
Block, William 88, 126-7
Blomfield, Arthur W. 93
Blomfield, Charles (Bishop of London)   62, 63, 71, 80
Booth family 90n5
Brassel, Philip (Rector) 105, 108
Brett, James 94
Britton, John 15
Brooks, James 93, 94, 96, 97, 106, 110n50
Brown, Cecil 105, 107, 108
BTCV (British Trust for Conservation Volunteers) 115
Buckley, Samuel 53, 54
Buckton, George 67, 74n10
Bumpstead, John 67
Butterfield, William 92
Byrdsong Choir 120

C
Cameron, Neil 108
Campbell, Peter 110n31
Candish, (Cavendish) Richard 39, 101, 110n63
Cansick, Frederick Teague 87
Capon, William 31
Carlos, Edward John 19, 20 n19, 22, 27, 30, 31, 61
Carter, John 49
Carter, Robert 51, 52, 126-7
Cartwright, Thomas (Rector) 48, 49, 59n4
Cave, Mrs. C. M. 103
Chambers, Elizabeth 53, 54
Chapman, Edward 90n5
Chapman (Schapman) Robert, ... 25, 32
Chatelain, Jean-Baptiste-Claude 11, 12
Cherry, Bridget 120n4, n7

Chivers, Derek 35, 37, 38
Cibber, Caius Gabriel 44, 45
City Charities Fund 98
Clay, Richard 110n27
Cleary, Frederick 103, 110n37
Clennell, J. 9
Cliveden Conservation 120n10
Cokke, Henry 25
Collcutt, A. W. 16
Cole, William (Rector) 24, 33, 35, 47-53, 48
Collier, Giles 41
Colquhoun, Frances 120n7
Cooke, George 16
Corlette, H. C. 96
Council for the Care of Churches 99
Couse, Kenton 54
Crawley, George 110n27
Creighton, Mandell (Bishop of London) 96, 97
Crump, Reginald Peter 100
Crump, W. H. 100
Cumberland, Margaret Countess of 39
Cutbush, William and Son 95

D
Dalton, John 41
Dickens, Charles 84, 90n20
Dickens, Charles Scrase 90n5
Dicker, Elizabeth 59
Diocesan Advisory Committee
(DAC) 105, 106, 109, 110n48
Draper, F.W.M. 110n36
Draper, Roger 42

E
Edward VI, King 34
Eeles, F. C. 99
English Heritage 111, 120n9
Evans, David 77

F
Ferrey, Benjamin 80, 81, 90n11
Fincham, Edgar 99
Fisher, Thomas 19, 20n18, 30, 37, 53, 54, 61
Flitcroft, Henry 54
Friends of Hornsey Church Tower 112, 115-9
Frith, David W. 106
Fox, Alan 120n13, 126-7

G
Gant, Frederick James 110n27
Gay, Ken 120n4
George V, King 100
Gillman, H. A. 82
Godfrey, Abraham 42
Gough, Richard 13
Griffin, G. 94
Grindal, Edmund (Bishop of London) 36
Groves, Mr. 74n10

129

H

Haghe, L.	80
Halsey, Edward	53
Hands, Benjamin	110n27
Haringey, Borough of	105, 120n9, n14
Haringey Council	115-6
Harrington, Robert (Rector)	36, 37, 41, 46n5
Harvey, Richard (Rector)	62-6, 63, 78, 80, 90n7, 91, 99
Hassell, John	17
Haultain, Francis (Rector)	54, 60n20
Hawksmoor, Nicholas	66, 104
Haygarth, Revd. Richard	64, 74n10
Heritage Lottery Fund	120n9
Heritage of London Trust	115, 120n14
Hibberd, Shirley	83
Highgate Wood School	121
Hill, John	28, 32, 34
Hippolite, F.G.	105
Hornsey Borough Council	95
Hornsey Conservation Area Advisory Committee (HCAAC)	111
Hornsey District Council	95
Hornsey Guild	95
Hornsey Historical Society	111, 120n4
Hornsey Temperance Society	97
Howley, William (Bishop of London and Archbishop of Canterbury)	90n5

I

Incorporated Church Building Society (ICBS) 62, 65, 77, 92

J

James, Col. Edward	53, 54
Jannaway, Thomas	55
Jeakes, James (Rector)	91, 92, 94, 97
Johnston, Hilda	112
Jukes, Francis	13
Juxon, William (Bishop of London)	41

K

Kempe, Charles Eamer	97
Knox, John	36

L

Lant, Thomas (Rector)	41, 42, 43, 46n.28
Laud, William (Bishop of London and Archbishop of Canterbury)	40, 41, 43
Laurence King & Partners	107
Linzee, Revd. Edward	101
Lloyd, Thomas (Rector)	52
Lolocks, Robert	28, 32
London Diocesan Fund	104
London, Geoffrey (Galfrid)	25, 32
London, John	32
Long, George	86
Long, Harriet	86, 126-7
Lucas, Mr	74n10
Lysons, Daniel	14, 30, 53

M

Mansfield, Lord	90n5
Marshall, Richard D	110n27
Marshall, William	55
Martin, John	94
Mary, Queen	34, 36
McGregor, Mr.	95
Mears and Stainbank	100
Mears, Thomas	71
Metropolitan Building Fund	63
Middlesex County Association	95
Middlesex Regiment	97-8, 104, 107
Midwinter, Daniel	48, 59n3, 87, 90n27
Mihill, Mr	56
Mitchell family	60, n22, 126-7
Montgomery Campbell, Henry (Rector, later Bishop of London)	98, 110n48
Moody, John C.	103
Morgan family	56, 59n7, 116, 126-7
Musters family	43, 45, 46n39
Musters, Francis	44, 45, 78, 101, 109, 110n63
Musters, Jane	45, 46n45, 101
Musters, Lady	43
Musters, Sir John	44

N

Nicholson, Sir Charles	96
Norden, John	26
North Middlesex Family History Society	87, 111, 116

P

Packer, Thomas	82, 83
Parsons, Mary	59
Pattinson, William	86, 87, 120, 126-7
Parochial Church Council (PCC)	107, 112
Paul, John William	58
Peacock, Mark Beauchamp	88, 126-7
Phillips, Joseph (?)	51, 59n9
Piper, Thomas and Son	66, 73
Piper, Thomas II	66
Poole, Henry	54
Pott, Henry	58, 126-7
Poulton, William	88-89, 126-7
Prattent, Thomas	21
Price, Thomas	110n27
Prickett, George	63, 74n10
Priestley, Thomas	38
Priestley, William	38, 99
Prynne, G. H. Fellowes	98
Pugin, Auguste	80
Pugin, A. W. N.	80, 92

R

Reed, A. R.	104
Rey, George	35, 38, 39, 61, 101, 109
Rey, George (jun.)	39, 40
Reynolds, John	49
Richards, J. H. Melville	103

Richardson, Anthony 112, 120
Roberts, J. 12
Robins, Gilbert 94, 95
Robinson, William 79
Roffe, Edwin 84
Rogers, Charles 67, 74n10, 110n27
Rogers, John 110n27
Rogers, Samuel 78, 84, 95, 101, 116, 117, 125
Rooker, Michael 'Angelo' 15
Ross, C.H. 95
Royal Commission on Historical Monuments   110n32
Royal Cumberland Youths 94
Rug(ge)vale, John 25, 32
Ruggevale, Richard 32

S

Sackville, Thomas 45
Sadleir, Thomas 67, 74n10
Saintsbury, Peter 107
Sandby, Paul 15
Sanders, Peter 120n4, *122*
Savage, Thomas (Bishop of London) 14, 29
Schnebbelie, Robert 14
Schwitzer, Joan 112, 115, 120n13, 126-7
Seabrook, Geoffrey (Rector) 108, 111, 120n13, *122*
Seaton, Joseph 51, 52
Sedding, John Dando 96
Schnebbelie, Robert 14
Shepherd, Charles (Rector) 57, 62
Sheppard, Hilda 98
Sherlock, Thomas (Bishop of London) 48
Sidey, C. J. M. 98, 100
Skevington (Skeffington), John 32
Skevington, Sir John 33
Skevington family 38
Smith family 59n7, 126-7
Smith, George
 64-6, 68, 71, 72, 73, 75, 76, 79, 80, 91, 93, 99, 100, 103
Smith, John Thomas 17
Smith, Joshua Toulmin 87-8, 126-7
Snell, William 88, 126-7
Society for the Protection of Ancient Buildings
 (SPAB) 104
Sperling, J. H. 81
Stationers' Company 59n3, 87
Stockdale, Frederick William Lichfield 15, 16
Suley, Judith 51, 126-7
Sweetapple, Penelope 59n6

T

Taylor family 85
Taylor, J. H. 85
Temple, Frederick (Bishop of London) 93
Territt, John (Rector) 52
Thatcher, William 43
Thicknesse, Francis N. (Rector) 97
Thomson, William 28
Thompson, W. H. 89
Thorne, James 83, 84
Thornton, William 10, 11
Towers, C. W. 77
Towers, Hannah 53, 60n14, 101, 126-7
Towers, Samuel 49, 53
Towers, William Samuel 58
Townshend, Mr. 74n10
Turvey, Robert 32

V

Van de Linde Monteuuis, Gerard 88, 116, 126-7
Victoria and Albert Museum 44, 110n63
Victoria, Queen 97
Viney, Mr. 74n10
Vulliamy, Lewis 65, 74n21

W

Wade, Thomas 54
Walker, I. 13
Walker, Jacob 86, 116, 126-7
Walker, William 52
Walton, W. L. 82
Ware family 58, 126-7
War Salvage Campaign 100
Warham, William
 (Bishop of London, Archbishop of Canterbury)   14, 29
Warner estate 91
Warner, Eliza 79, 101
Warner, George 71
Warner, Henry 67, 71, 74n10, 79, 126-7
Warner, Jacob 79, 101
Warner, John, and Sons 94
Watson, John James 62
Watson, Joshua 62
Westfield, Thomas (Rector) 40
Whitechapel Bell Foundry 71, 100, 104, 107
Willarton, Robert (Rector) 36
Willis, Henry, and Sons 97
Winston, S. 41
Wollaston, Sir John 41
Worley, Mr. 74n10

ILLUSTRATION CREDITS

The author and publishers are grateful to the following for permission to produce material in their possession.

Anthony Richardson Architects:
7.24, 8.1, 8.2, 8.3, 8.6

The Bodleian Libraries, University of Oxford:
1.6

Trustees of the British Museum, Department of Prints and Drawings:
1.7, 1.12, 3.14, 3.17, 4.1, 4.5, 4.6, 4.17, 6.8, 6.9, 6.11, 6.12, 6.13, 6.14, 6.16, 6.17, 6.18, 6.19, 7.2

Bruce Castle Museum, Culture Libraries and Learning:
1.5, 1.17, 2.2, 2.22, 3.8, 4.13, 4.15, 4.16, 5.1, 5.11, 6.1, 6.15

Derek Chivers:
3.4, 3.7

Frances Colquhoun:
8.13, 8.16, 8.18, P2, P6, P12, P14, P17, p.125

Historic England:
3.6, 3.10, 7.4, 7.7, 7.8, 7.9, 7.12, 7.13, 7.14, 7.15

Hornsey Historical Society:
6.23, 6.28. 7.10

Hornsey Parish Church:
7.20, 7.22, 7.23

Lambeth Palace Library:
5.5, 5.6

London Metropolitan Archives:
1.2, 1.4, 1.8, 1.13, 1.16, 1.18, 2.21, 2.23, 3.3, 4.4, 5.2, 5.4, 5.7, 6.20

Museum of London:
5.9, 5.10

National Portrait Gallery:
1.15

Newport Art Gallery:
1.11

Peter Sanders:
2.9, 2.10, 2.11, 2.12, 2.13, 2.17, 3.2, 3.9, 3.12, 3.13, 4.10, 4.11, 4.14, 4.18, 4.19, 4.20, 4.21, 5.8, 5.18, 6.2, 6.4, 6.21, 6.22, 6.26, 7.3, 7.5abc, 7.11, 7.18, 7.19, P1, P4, P5, P7, P8, P9, P10, P11, P13, P16, P121(6) back cover

Rebecca Sheldon:
P15

SUBSCRIBERS TO IVY-MANTLED TOWER

Keith Fawkes-Underwood
Peter Barber OBE
Roy Hidson
Janet M. Owen
Albert Pinching
Hugh & Ruth Garnsworthy
Dr. Eleri Rowlands
Lesley Ramm
David Frith
David Dell
Chris Hannington
Beryl Gibbs
Ena Duffley
Anne M. Foley
Brenda Porter
Tony Hunt & Judith Filkin
Mark Cooke
Ludovic McRae
Dave Taylor
Patricia Kneen
Samuel Dill
Roger Kemp
Dr. Andrew Pink
Isobel & Malcolm Stokes
Pauline P. Lewis
W. T. Rees
Brenda Griffith-Williams
Jennifer Bell MBE
Professor Sandra Clark
Joyce Rosser
The late Marion Arnell-Wilton
J. A. H. Emery
Daphne Dell
Judy Harman
Catherine Kennally
Nicolas Allaway
Janice Williams

Anthony Richardson
The Jansons Road Historiographical & Horticultural Collective
Adrian Thomas
Margaret Hudson
Joy & Glen Nichol
Eleanor Hellier
Cllr. Viv Ross
Amanda Davidson
Peter Thompson
Florence St John Heller
Robert Rust
Bill Tyler
Mercy Cleland
Stephen Driver
Ann Jones
Alan Nafzger
Nancy Rossi
Marion Turner
Stephen Rigg
Muswell Hill & Fortis Green Association
Glynn Davis
Mark Hilbert
Nigel Lingwood
R. W. L. Davies
Maureen Wenham
Revd. Patrick & Dr. Irena Henderson
Brenda Barwick
Albert & Christine Barnwell
Janet Barwani
John Eakins
Valerie Foulis
Ann Saunders

David Bevan
Steve King
Deborah Hedgecock
Frances Colquhoun
Peter Sanders
Dr. Linda Almond
Jill Letten
Margaret & Paul Walker
Dr. Simon Bradley
Liz & Mike Wood
E. W. Partridge
Tracey Clark-Edwards
Revd. Brooke Lunn
Tim McLean
William Hopper
Elizabeth Israel
John Gooding
John Mee
Kelyn Bacon Darwin
Lesley Hales
Richard Holmes
Bracewells Estate Agents
PhilipAlexander Estate Agents
Prickett & Ellis Estate Agents
Jeff Boudens
Pauline Green
Rachael Macdonald
Ruth Hazeldine
Stephen Hoyle
Barbara Connell
Rosemary Carter
Stephen Whittle
Rosalind Abrams
Eric Snape
David Winskill